NEVER GIVE UP

NEVER GIVE UP

GIVE UP

Seven Principles for
Christian Leaders in Tough Times

SCOTT DICKSON with TRACY SUMNER

BARBOUR
PUBLISHING

Cover design by Greg Jackson, Jackson Design Co, LLC

Published by Barbour Publishing, Inc., P.O. Box 719, Uhrichsville, Ohio 44683
www.barbourbooks.com

Our mission is to publish and distribute inspirational products offering exceptional value and biblical encouragement to the masses.

ecpa Member of the
Evangelical Christian
Publishers Association

Printed in the United States of America.
5 4 3 2 1

Dedicated to my lovely and wise wife, Priscilla,
and to my much-loved sons, David, Patrick, and Daniel.

CONTENTS

"God doesn't deliver us from trouble.

God delivers us in trouble."

OSWALD CHAMBERS

"Hope has two beautiful daughters;

anger and courage:

anger at the way things are,

and courage to struggle to create things

as they should be."

SAINT AUGUSTINE OF HIPPO

"Have I not commanded you?

Be strong and courageous!

Do not tremble or be dismayed,

for the LORD your God is with you wherever you go."

JOSHUA 1:9 NASB

INTRODUCTION

Many years ago, Winston Churchill, the British prime minister, by then well along in years, was invited to speak at the graduation exercises at Harrow School, a prestigious private school located in northwest London. As he was introduced to the students, he was described not only as one of the greatest leaders and statesmen of the twentieth century but also as a great speaker.

No doubt, the students and others in attendance that day were expecting a brilliant address from one of the greatest speakers of their time. What they heard, however, was certainly the shortest and simplest speech Churchill ever delivered—*and* the most memorable.

Churchill took the podium, faced the audience, and said, "Never give up. Let me continue by saying: Never, never give up! And in conclusion, I say to you: Never, never, never give up!" Churchill then returned to his seat as the audience came to its feet in thunderous applause.

Churchill knew well the importance of not giving up, even in the face of what seemed like overwhelming odds. In what historians consider one of the finest hours of any world leader, he had brilliantly led Great Britain through the darkest time in the history of the nation, the Nazi invasion of the homeland during World War II.

At the age of sixty-five, Churchill replaced Neville

11

Chamberlain as British prime minister, and he did so as the United Kingdom faced certain attack by Nazi forces. Shortly after he took office, Belgium and France surrendered to Germany, and it appeared that Great Britain was next. In July 1940, the German air force began bombing British shipping and ports, and in September, the people of London began enduring nightly air raids by the Nazis.

In the midst of the attacks, Churchill defiantly showed up at the bombing sites, often flashing the two-fingered "V for victory" salute for all to see. This was Churchill's way of encouraging and emboldening the British people and their military forces. It sent the clear message that Churchill was not going to allow them to give up, no matter how bad things got. His leadership in a time when things seemed hopeless kept the people united and the military fighting, and eventually Great Britain defeated the Nazi forces.

While Churchill's words and deeds changed the course of history, they were far from the first encouraging people to persevere—to "never give up"—even in the face of what seemed overwhelming opposition. Jesus gave those who place their faith in Him essentially that very same encouragement when He made us two promises: "In the world you have tribulation, but take courage; I have overcome the world" (John 16:33 NASB).

God never promised His people an easy life, a life free from tests, trials, and even failures. What He *does* promise, however, is that He is bigger than anything we have to face in this life. Furthermore, He gave us this promise: "Be strong and courageous, do not be afraid or tremble. . .for the LORD your God is the one who goes with you. He will not fail you or forsake you" (Deuteronomy 31:6 NASB).

The scriptures are chock-full of examples of God's interventions in what appear to be impossible situations. From the stories of Adam and Eve, Noah, and Abraham in the book of Genesis to the account of His ultimate intervention in a world gone mad as recorded in the book of Revelation, we have promise upon fulfilled promise of God stepping into and intervening in people's lives and situations and showing the way forward.

Here's the good news for us today: He's still doing the very same thing.

But does that include the business world? Does God want to be involved in our earthly businesses—even in the tough times? Absolutely! God makes it abundantly clear that He wants to be involved in *every* area of our lives, that He wants to stand beside us in all things and redeem *any* situation, no matter how "dark" it may be.

Most of us have no trouble believing that God is personally and intimately involved in the affairs of great world leaders as well as the men and women He has called to do great things for Him in ministry. But many of us have a hard time buying into the idea that God has either the time or the inclination to become involved in the affairs of our earthly businesses. But I believe that He wants to do just that, if we do but two things: honor Him in how we do our business, and *never give up*!

As of this writing, I have spent thirty years in the business world, including fifteen in the ultracompetitive airline industry. During this time, God has provided me with many opportunities to demonstrate His compassion, love, and power at every level of my business. And, more important, He's continually reminded me that He's always with me, helping me through the good times, the tough times, and even the failures.

After three decades of serving and trusting God in my business, I am convinced that He wants to do great things in our business and personal lives, *if* we would only ask Him. For that reason, I can confidently say that I will continue to trust God in my business—no matter how difficult times become—and that I will *never give up*!

I have written this book with the goal of demonstrating what I believe are God-given principles for leadership. Specifically, the principles covered in the following chapters are designed to show the reader practical dimensions of leading through even the most difficult of business—or everyday life—situations.

This book is by no means a complete compendium of "how-tos" when it comes to leading during tough times. No two business situations are the same, simply because different people and different business climates are involved. But it is my hope that the principles and suggestions in this book will open your eyes, mind, and heart to all that God can do in the stressful, up-and-down world of business.

While many of the principles I have presented in this book come from the perspective of a person in leadership, they are also applicable at all levels of a working life. Whether you are the CEO, janitor, clerk, midlevel manager, or self-employed entrepreneur, the power of God and the "tools" He gives to lead us can transform our lives and our businesses. I have seen these things work in my own business life. As I rose through the ranks in my career, I found that the leadership principles I used as an airline CEO are just as relevant and just as effective as when I used them as an entry-level research analyst for the local bus company in Minneapolis–St. Paul, Minnesota.

This book is not the story of one specific business or event. However, in writing this book, I acknowledge that the events of September 11, 2001, and their aftermath brought the principles outlined in these chapters into much clearer focus.

Having gone through those experiences has brought me to a place where I can offer you, the reader, the insights contained in this book and to where I can confidently encourage anyone facing challenges to do two things: Trust in God, and *never give up*!

SETTING THE SCENE

*"In the world you have tribulation,
but take courage;
I have overcome the world."*

JOHN 16:33 NASB

THE VANGUARD AIRLINES FLIGHT

from Kansas City to New York City's LaGuardia Airport broke through the overcast sky just over the southern tip of Manhattan Island. As the old MD-80 broke through the clouds, the pilot, Captain Ed King, and I remarked almost simultaneously how beautiful the Twin Towers of the World Trade Center looked that early morning. The magnificent skyscrapers, both stretching 1,350 feet from the city streets, towered peacefully above the rest of the island, beautifully illuminated against the Manhattan skyline.

At the time, I had been serving for about five months as president and CEO of Vanguard Airlines, a small carrier based in Kansas City, Missouri. Vanguard had struggled badly before I assumed leadership, and it desperately needed an infusion of new capital, so our primary shareholder and I were in New York for a series of meetings with some potential investors. Vanguard had been doing better financially in the few months prior to my trip to New York, and I was feeling very hopeful that it would be a fruitful trip.

As was often my practice when I took a Vanguard flight, I spent the last hour of the trip riding in the cockpit, chatting with the crew. The flight was running nearly three hours late, a typical delay going into New York under the circumstances. In the previous twelve hours, thunderstorms had severely disrupted air traffic on the East Coast—an all-too-common occurrence, as most frequent air travelers know—and nearly every flight going out of and coming into the Big Apple was delayed.

Our approach into LaGuardia took us on a horseshoe-shaped path north along the Hudson River, parallel to Manhattan, then back to the southeast for what commercial pilots know can be a tricky landing. After the flight was on the ground, I gathered my bags and headed to a Manhattan hotel to catch a few hours' sleep. It was already close to 2 a.m., and I wanted to be well rested for that day's meetings with the investors.

That day was Tuesday, September 11, 2001.

A Rude Awakening

I awoke later that morning rested and ready to take on our presentations. I showered, dressed, then spent some time reading my Bible and praying. I hadn't turned on the radio or the television in my room. Just as I was about to call our majority stockholder, Rich (Rich has asked that his full name not be included in this book), the phone rang. It was Rich.

I expected to talk with Rich about coordinating the

events of the day, which included our first meeting at 10 a.m. Rich, however, had something else on his mind, something that would shake the world, including the world of the airline industry, to its very core.

"Scott, you'd better turn on your TV," Rich said. "Something big is happening. There has been some kind of plane crash."

A plane crash of any kind is always a major concern for someone in the airline industry, so I immediately turned on the television in my hotel room. I was horrified at what I saw.

Huge clouds of smoke poured from near the top of the World Trade Center's north tower. As I listened to the news report, I learned that an airliner had indeed crashed into the tower. At first, I thought it was some kind of terrible accident. My mind went to an incident in 1945, near the end of World War II, when a B-25 bomber crashed into the Empire State Building, then the world's tallest building.

But I soon realized that this was no accident. As I continued watching, at just after 9 a.m. eastern standard time, a second plane struck the south tower. I knew then that our nation was under some kind of attack.

> My hotel was a little over a mile from the World Trade Center, but all my wife knew that morning was that I was in a Manhattan hotel. She had no way of knowing whether or not I was a safe distance from the now-burning Twin Towers.

Later, I, along with the rest of the world, learned that Muslim extremists had hijacked a pair of planes—American

Flight 11 and United Flight 175, both out of Boston—and crashed them into the towers. In addition, another flight—American Airlines Flight 77—had been hijacked and crashed into the side of the Pentagon in Washington, D.C. A fourth doomed flight—United Airlines Flight 93—had been hijacked and headed east from Pennsylvania but had crashed before reaching its target.

At that moment, I felt more numbed than fearful. It hit me almost instantly that my wife, Priscilla, would be very worried about me, so I tried to call her to let her know that I was safe. My hotel was a little over a mile from the World Trade Center, but all my wife knew that morning was that I was in a Manhattan hotel. She had no way of knowing whether or not I was a safe distance from the now-burning Twin Towers.

I dialed our home number several times—on the hotel phone and on my cell phone—but I couldn't get through on either. I then tried to call my office, hoping someone there could contact Priscilla for me. Again, no success. Apparently, the phone lines were tied up by people calling into and out of New York City.

I called Rich so we could figure out what to do next. Rich, like many Americans by this time, was enraged at what had happened. His thoughts were about finding out who was responsible for this atrocity and about what kind of retribution we as a nation should mete out. My thoughts, however, were on Vanguard's planes and the people who operated them. I wondered if they were all safely on the ground.

Neither of us knew quite what to do, so we decided to go ahead and make our appearance at our first meeting. We arranged to meet in the hotel lobby, and I hung up the phone and prepared to leave my room. But just as I was about to walk out the door around 10:00, I heard the news on the television that the Pentagon had been hit and that all United States flights had been grounded.

As I left my room and headed toward the hotel lobby, all kinds of thoughts raced through my mind. I thought about the people who had lost their lives in the attack and about the implications for our country. I also thought about what this all would mean to the airline industry, particularly to Vanguard and its employees. Our airline had been just scraping by financially, and I knew that any interruption in our ability to fly would likely put us in dire straits.

And I thought about my son, David, who had been in China for the past several months teaching English as a second language. He was scheduled to fly home that very morning.

Rich and I met in the hotel lobby, then walked up Park Avenue from our midtown Manhattan hotel to the site of that first meeting. As you might expect, it wasn't a very productive time as far as our presentation was concerned. All of us were at a loss for words, at least when it came to discussing investments in Vanguard Airlines. All we could think or talk about was the people we knew who had offices at the World Trade Center and about implications of the attack for the airline industry.

After our meeting, Rich and I headed for the street and

hurried back to our hotel. Our journey back was against a flood of people streaming north away from the towers, which by then had collapsed. It was an unforgettable scene. A dense cloud of smoke hovered in the south from the towers, and there was an acrid odor in the air. As we made our way across town, we saw tens of thousands of terrified people lining every north-south street we passed. People in cars, taxis, and buses, as well as those on bikes and on foot, fled lower Manhattan and the vicinity of the World Trade Center towers as fast as they could. I was struck not only by the number of people I saw fleeing but by how orderly they did so.

When I returned to the hotel, I immediately checked to see if the phones were working. They were, so I called home. As I knew she would be, my wife was extremely worried about me. To this day, the conversation remains a blur. I remember telling Priscilla that I was about a mile from the World Trade Center and that I was safe. And I remember asking her about our son. I was grateful and relieved to learn that he had arrived home about five that morning.

I knew that the following weeks and months would be like none I had ever experienced in my professional life.

Priscilla and I assured one another of our love and prayers, and after we hung up, I called the Vanguard corporate office to let the people there know that I was okay. They, too, were relieved to hear from me. As I talked to several of the company's officers, I learned that the Federal Aviation Administration (FAA) had ordered the immediate grounding of all aircraft in the United States. I was amazed and thankful to learn that when the cease-flying order came, all but one of our planes was already on the ground at our home base. That one other aircraft was safely on the ground in Atlanta. Our flight from LaGuardia back to Kansas City had left New York on schedule that morning, about ninety minutes before the chaos started, and had already reached its destination.

As I finished my conversations with the people at the office and hung up the phone, the reality of our situation began to set in. I knew that the following weeks and months would be like none I had ever experienced in my professional life. It was during that time that I would have to apply everything I'd learned about corporate leadership.

DEALING WITH THE AFTERMATH

The few days following the terrorist attacks passed in a blur. I was away from my home base in Kansas City, but I was still busy. I operated a pseudo command center out of my hotel room in New York, conferring regularly with my staff about all the new security directives the FAA and other government bodies had handed down. It seemed that we were receiving new directives every few hours, which only added to the stress of dealing with the events of the past few days.

During those times when I ventured outside the hotel, I saw a lower Manhattan that looked and sounded eerily different from what it had looked and sounded like just a few days earlier. If you've ever been on the streets of Manhattan during the busy part of a typical day, you know that they are usually teeming with many thousands of people heading in all directions. But this, of course, was not a typical day. The streets were nearly empty and it was much quieter than usual. About the only sounds I heard were of military aircraft flying overhead, barely above the tops of the New York City skyscrapers.

On Thursday of that week, two days after the attack, the FAA's cease-flying order was partially lifted, and I was able to board Rich's private plane and fly from New York back to Kansas City. My secretary picked me up at the general aviation terminal at Kansas City International, which was only a few minutes from Vanguard's offices.

When I walked into the Vanguard Airlines office, I was met by the greetings of officers and staff members, who were all greatly relieved that I was safely home, and by what seemed like an unending string of questions about what I'd seen and heard. Rather than repeat the story a dozen times, I gathered our officers and key staff into my office to talk to them about my experience and what it meant to all of us.

> Now, we would be faced with the daunting task of reaccommodating thousands of passengers with new flights. The job would be herculean.

When I called that meeting, I did so knowing that our airline (like all other commercial carriers) faced incredible and immediate challenges. We would have to deal with the needs of our employees as well as the needs of hundreds of customers stranded at our hub in Kansas City and elsewhere around our network.

That morning, I heard all kinds of questions but had few immediate answers. Where would our stranded customers stay and how long would they be stranded? When would the FAA allow us to resume flying? What kind of future does Vanguard Airlines face?

Fortunately, one of those questions was answered the following day, when the FAA allowed airlines to resume flying. Now, we would be faced with the daunting task of reaccommodating thousands of passengers with new flights. The job would be herculean, but the Vanguard employees were up to it, and within a few days the backlog of customers was cleared out and people got where they needed to be.

While we were successful in our efforts to serve our passengers in the wake of the September 11 attacks, we at Vanguard still faced mounting stress and never-ending questions over the following days, weeks, and months.

AN INDUSTRY IN CHAOS

The terrorist attacks did significant damage to the American economy, already headed into a recession at the time, and we in the airline industry felt that damage immediately.

In the days following the attacks, the industry as a whole

lost millions of dollars a day as people, many afraid to board a flight and many facing uncertainty in their own financial lives, mostly stopped buying tickets. The airline industry is what is called a "cash-flow business," meaning that most airlines rely heavily on daily cash disbursements from sales made on Web sites, through reservation centers, and through travel agencies. With this cash flow mostly dried up, airlines struggled to pay employees, contractors, and vendors of key services, such as fuel companies. All of us in the industry knew that the loss of any of a number of key vendors' services would cause a shutdown of all or part of our networks.

At Vanguard, dramatically reduced sales, customer service issues prompted by the security regulations, vendor demands for payments, and an enormous reduction in the desire of investors to put money into any airline—let alone one like Vanguard, which had a history of financial difficulties—became both daily and long-term issues.

When It All Ended

Over the ten months that followed the terrorist attacks, Vanguard struggled greatly but continued its operations. By the summer of 2002, however, the airline's financial situation worsened. We were in the midst of a good summer season; ticket sales were up dramatically. But a bizarre combination of events occurred, events that would lead to the end of Vanguard.

Around 95 percent of Vanguard's ticket sales were done

through credit card transactions. The banks that processed many of these sales began to become nervous about our financial situation (we were literally surviving day to day) and required changes in the way those

> In a very real sense, our own success was killing us.

transactions were collateralized—that is, protected against potential default by the airline. The banks increased our level of collateralization, which meant that for every dollar we brought in through bank card sales, they held back about $1.20 of our future sales. We were, despite our high level of sales at the time, in a negative cash-flow situation.

This had been an ongoing crisis for some months, but it hit a peak in the summer as our sales volume shot up. The more we sold, the more the credit card processors sought collateral. In a very real sense, our own success was killing us. We were in deep financial trouble. Our shareholders could not provide more capital, and the U.S. government refused to provide a loan guarantee.

In nearly three decades in the transportation industry, I had never experienced such an unusual juxtaposition of financial events. This pushed Vanguard to the brink of bankruptcy. Finally, on July 28, 2002, our board and senior staff agreed that we had no choice but to suspend operations and file for protection under Chapter 11.

July 29 was one of the most miserable days of my life. We had to face the media and we had to announce the bankruptcy to our eleven hundred employees—people I cared for personally, people who would, at least temporarily, be losing their livelihoods—and to our frustrated and greatly inconvenienced customers. We also had to alert our shareholders, who would be facing the loss of their financial investments in Vanguard, and to our vendors and suppliers, who would also suffer loss.

LESSONS FROM A BUSINESS FAILURE

I was heartbroken over the demise of Vanguard Airlines. But at the same time, I saw up close and personally how applying the principles of leading in difficult times can make times of struggle and even failure times when God does great things in and through us.

I saw how God's plan involves the building of character, faith, and a life of prayer in the Christian leader and how building those things within us sometimes means going through difficult times. But I also saw how when He builds these qualities within us, He also prepares us for the next test and for the next assignment. In so doing, He shows us how to persevere and how to deal with tough times and the stress those tough times always bring with them.

Read on, and you will see how Christian leaders can persevere and overcome—in the best of times and in the most difficult of times.

PRINCIPLE 1:

PUT FEAR IN ITS PLACE

"Have I not commanded you?
Be strong and courageous.
Do not be terrified; do not be discouraged,
for the LORD your God will be with you wherever you go."

JOSHUA 1:9

ON SATURDAY, MARCH 4,
1933, during his first inaugural address, United States president-elect Franklin Delano Roosevelt told a frightened and discouraged nation, "The only thing we have to fear is fear itself."

The nation had plenty of cause for fear and discouragement at that time in history. The American people, as well as those in most of the rest of the world, were suffering through what has been dubbed "the Great Depression."

Roosevelt took office at one of the worst points of the Depression, which was precipitated by, among other factors, the Wall Street stock market crash of late October 1929. The horrendous economic downturn that followed the crash devastated the nation. Thirteen million Americans—roughly one-quarter of the workforce—were unemployed, and by the time Roosevelt won election, many had literally been without work for years. The stock market was in shambles, and many banks, as well as other financial institutions, had simply shut down. Farms and other businesses fell into bankruptcy.

Times were brutally tough, and few saw hope for improvement in the near future. To make matters worse for many people, there was at the time no "safety net" for those out of work and desperate just to feed, clothe, and house their families. People could rely only on themselves.

Franklin Roosevelt had a plan for bringing the nation out of the Great Depression. But he understood that no plan was going to make the kind of difference that needed to be made if the people remained so paralyzed with fear that they couldn't move forward.

> It truly amazes me when I meet business leaders who actually seem to look for reasons to be afraid of moving forward.

No matter what you think of Roosevelt's "New Deal" and the effects it has had on culture, the economy, and politics in America, it's hard not to agree that fear is the first and foremost enemy we need to overcome if we want to move forward and do bigger and better things.

FEAR: WHAT IT LOOKS LIKE

There are many different kinds of fear, and some of them are healthy and beneficial to us. For example, we need to have a certain measure of fear when we cross a busy street on foot. In other words, we need to have a fear of being hit by a car so that we can take the appropriate steps to make sure that doesn't happen.

In this chapter, however, I want to address what I consider *destructive* fear, the kind of fear that inhibits us from being what God intends for us to be in all areas of our lives, including business. This is the kind of fear that paralyzes us when it's time to make a difficult decision, the kind of fear that gives us unneeded stress and anxiety, the kind that keeps us from moving forward and doing bigger and better things.

It truly amazes me when I meet business leaders who actually seem to *look* for reasons to be afraid of moving forward. They're afraid of change, afraid of risk, and afraid of fear itself. That kind of fear can be crippling to a leader, and it can be death to his or her company or corporation, especially in difficult times. That's because it is virtually impossible to avoid "fearful" situations, especially in today's business climate, where mergers, acquisitions, failures, and restructurings have become the norm.

Fear and stress are so closely linked that they feed off of one another and "enable" one another to have free run in our lives. By that, I mean that fear breeds stress, and stress is sustained by fear. Fear greatly limits us, both in our personal lives and in our corporate lives. Fear keeps the stress levels higher than they need to be and detracts from the sound thinking and strong corporate leadership it takes to get a company through the hard times.

I believe this kind of fear is at least partially to blame for the kind of climate that has given rise to the WorldComs and Enrons—scandals that rocked our early twenty-first-century business and financial worlds, costing investors and taxpayers many billions of dollars—of the business world. Of course, simple greed had a lot to do with those scandals, but fear—for example, fear of not meeting or exceeding shareholder expectations, a huge issue in the era of publicly owned companies and corporations—can also bring business leaders to engage in illegal and immoral business attitudes and practices.

Fear may not always cause business leaders to engage in immoral or illegal practices, but it will almost always cause people to make bad decisions or, worse yet, to make no decision at all. Fear keeps the business leader from making tough decisions or taking risks—both of which, as any successful leader knows, are keys to success in the business world.

This can often happen when the leader is "frozen" over fear of something that hasn't happened or that may not happen at all. This is what I call the "fear of the theys." More often than not, this is a fear of change and a fear of paradigms and programs a leader doesn't want to deal with, and not of actual people, events, or issues that have the potential to inhibit progress or damage a business.

At various times in my career, I have had the opportunity to work as an advisor to international airlines. One of the biggest problems I run into in my work with airline senior management is the managers' fear of people and fear of change. These managers consistently tell me that they cannot adopt the program or change in operations that I have suggested. These are tried-and-true programs and changes that I have personally seen bear much fruit in the industry—but contested because the elusive "they" will not like it.

Here is one example of this kind of fear in my own business life.

WRESTLING WITH FEAR

I recently served as a senior-level advisor to the new owner and president of an airline in a South American country. One of my responsibilities was assisting the airline in modernizing its information technology capabilities, which would help the airline compete better with the more technologically advanced carriers serving the same region.

As part of my work with this airline, I came into contact with its information technology director (ITD), a capable man from a technical viewpoint but a man who had a limited view of "newer" technology options available to the airline. The reason? He had dealt with only one technology vendor. The incumbent vendor provided good software solutions and was certainly an acceptable choice in many respects, but there were problems with the professional relationship between the airline and the vendor.

One of my tasks was to upgrade the airline's revenue management capability. In other words, I would use my experience and expertise on software systems that help the airline increase revenues from its existing customer base by more effectively and judiciously controlling what seats were sold—at a given price and time—between any two pairs of cities. This dimension of airline revenue enhancement is known as *yield management*.

I was confident that more effectively applied yield management software tools could easily increase this airline's revenue by at least 5 percent from its existing

From the outset, it was clear to me that the ITD and I were not on the same page when it came to choosing between the two vendors.

customer base. Having had extensive experience with software vendors, I also knew that there were alternatives to the incumbent vendor who had supplied the airline with other software.

I spoke at length with the airline's staff about their options and helped the appropriate staff members solicit bids from the two most likely candidate vendors. In addition, I prepared a detailed critique of the bids and of the vendors. One of those vendors was the airline's current software system provider (the incumbent), and the other was a smaller company that specialized in yield management systems.

My analysis of the software systems and of the bidders showed me that the smaller company was clearly the better choice for this airline. While both offered comparable systems, the new vendor had superior training capability, an efficient installation process, and outstanding ongoing support. The new vendor also offered a slightly better price than the incumbent. I knew that by selecting the new vendor, the airline would be up and running faster, meaning it would generate revenue benefits much more quickly.

From the outset, it was clear to me that the ITD and I were not on the same page when it came to choosing between the two vendors. I found this rather curious for two reasons. First of all, I had purchased, installed, and used both systems in real-world situations—not to mention that at one point in my career, I had been on the staff of a major developer of yield management software—while the ITD had never purchased, installed, or used a yield management system of any kind. Secondly, the relationship between the airline and the incumbent vendor was not in a good place. The vendor had grown lackadaisical in its treatment of my client and on several occasions had failed to heed the airline's requests for assistance and enhancements to products.

Finally, as the day of the decision came near, the ITD, the director responsible for revenue management, and I met with the airline's president to make a final choice between the two vendors. As the meeting started, the president asked me to wait outside his office while he conferred with his staff on the matter. After about twenty minutes, I was invited back into the office.

After I took my seat in the office, the airline's president looked at me and said, "These guys want the incumbent vendor. What do you say?"

In answering the president's very direct question, I pointed out that I had extensive experience working with the systems being offered and explained my rationale for choosing the smaller vendor. When the president finally made his decision between the two vendors, he agreed with me and chose the newer one.

With that, the decision was made, but there were some fears on the part of the ITD, who was clearly chagrined over the decision, that we needed to address. "Something sticks in my throat about this decision," he said in Spanish. When we pressed him to tell us what concerned him about the decision, the next thing out of his mouth was, "I am afraid that the incumbent vendor will not like me for selecting someone else."

There it was: Fear over something that hadn't yet happened—namely, a damaged relationship between the airline and the incumbent software vendor, a relationship that wasn't in good shape anyway—was keeping this talented and able man from moving forward and making a change, a change I was convinced was in the best interests of the company.

I explained that choosing the new vendor wouldn't necessarily be the end of the relationship between the airline and the old vendor. In fact, I believed that purchasing the software from the new vendor could be good for the long-term relationship between the airline and the old vendor. That is exactly what happened, too. The old vendor, now mindful of the competition it faced, improved its service to the airline, and the business relationship between the two actually improved. At the same time, the new vendor installed its software, and the airline reaped significant financial benefits.

In hindsight, I have come to realize that had the president of that airline and I allowed the ITD's fear to prevail in that decision, two things would have happened: The airline would have lost several million dollars of added revenue, and it would likely still be in a frustrating business relationship with the incumbent software provider. I also believe to this day that the experience taught the ITD not to fear the unknown and that it has made him a better manager.

My experience with this South American airline is an example of what can happen when business leaders overcome fear. To me, it is also an example of what can happen when I take some basic steps toward overcoming fear.

These steps have proven themselves helpful to me as I've fought my battles with fear, and I know they can be helpful to you, too.

STEPS TO VICTORY OVER FEAR

I've found that overcoming fear isn't a matter of just saying, "I refuse to be afraid." Of course, it's important to have that kind of mind-set when you are faced with the kinds of decisions good leadership requires you to make, particularly in difficult times. But over the course of my career, I've found that there are practical steps you can take to win your battle with fear.

Here are those steps:

Step 1: Take hold of the fact that God doesn't want you living in fear. The first step in overcoming fear is realizing that God does not want any of us to live in gripping, paralyzing fear. That's because He knows well that fear limits us and limits what He can do with us as leaders.

Joshua stands as one of the Bible's greatest examples of the need for leaders to overcome fear. Moses, Joshua's predecessor as the leader of God's people, the Israelites, was gone, and now it was time for Joshua to step up and lead—lead them through the wilderness, through military conflicts, and into the Promised Land.

It wasn't going to be easy, but Joshua was the man to do it. And why was he the man to do it? Because God had called him. But God not only called Joshua to lead, he gave him this little "pep talk" before sending him out:

> *After the death of Moses the servant of the* LORD, *the* LORD *said to Joshua son of Nun, Moses' aide: "Moses my servant is dead. Now then, you and all these people, get ready to cross the Jordan River into the land I am about to give to them—to the Israelites. I will give you every place where you set your foot, as I promised Moses. Your territory will extend from the desert to Lebanon, and from the great river, the Euphrates—all the Hittite country—to the Great Sea on the west. No one will be able to stand up against you all the days of your life. As I was with Moses, so I will be with you; I will never leave you nor forsake you.*

"Be strong and courageous, because you will lead these people to inherit the land I swore to their forefathers to give them."

JOSHUA 1:1–6

Now that doesn't sound like a call to a life of fear, does it? Far from it! In fact, this is God at His fear-conquering best. This is God saying very simply, "I've put you in this situation, and I'm going to be with you through the good times and the bad, and for that reason, you need to put your fears in their place."

God has never promised us as leaders a life free from difficulty. But He tells us very explicitly in His written Word that we are not to allow fear to rule our lives.

Step 2: Be honest with yourself—and with God—about your fears. Think back on your life as a leader, and ask yourself how many times fear has limited your effectiveness or kept you from meeting your potential in your personal and business life. Are you afraid of people? Afraid of change? Afraid of risk? Afraid of consequences? Afraid of dealing with the inevitable "downturns" in your business?

Most of us would have to acknowledge both that we feel fear and that we, too, often give in to it and allow it to limit us. I've seen that in the world of the airline industry, where there are many wonderful opportunities to work overseas. Many of my colleagues in the industry have been presented opportunities to work outside the boundaries of the United

States, but they were afraid to take that risk. It wasn't that they had anything against living and working in another country; rather, it was a matter of being afraid to take the risks such a move brings with it. Sadly, by giving in to the fear of moving overseas, these men and women have limited themselves professionally.

> But God redeems everything, including the years when I was afraid to move forward and upward in my career.

Fortunately, I was not afraid of taking those kinds of risks. I wanted to travel, so I've jumped at opportunities to work in other countries. But I must confess that fear has held me back during certain times in my career. For example, I believe now that early in my career, when I worked in the world of public transportation, fear inhibited me somewhat. In hindsight, I can see that I limited myself early in my career by staying too long in the world of public transportation. I believe that God moved me into the public transportation sector. But I also believe I stayed there too long, mostly because it was a "safe" environment in which to work. Although there is not a lot of "upside" to public-sector jobs—by that I mean that the opportunities to advance and to reach one's potential are limited—they are generally very secure.

But God redeems everything, including the years when I was afraid to move forward and upward in my career. And today, I know that even as I was "frozen" in the world of transportation, God was working to free me of my fear.

Back in the third and fourth chapters of the book of Exodus, we read about a man who was honest with God about his fears. God had called Moses to lead His people out of captivity in Egypt. But Moses had all kinds of excuses—and they were all rooted in fear—as to why he couldn't lead: He thought of himself as a "nobody" whom Pharaoh wouldn't listen to (3:11). He didn't think the people would believe or follow him (4:1). He wasn't that great with words (4:10).

Moses then told God that maybe, just maybe, it would be a good idea for Him to send someone else to lead. God's answer? "No! I'm sending you. You're going to face opposition and setbacks, and there are going to be times when you might be afraid. But you're going to succeed because I am with you."

When it comes to facing fear—and there is no doubt that sooner or later we will all have to face our share—honesty is by far the best policy. When we acknowledge to ourselves that we are afraid and when we confess our fears to God, we open the way for Him to calm our hearts by reminding us of one simple fact: He's there for us through everything.

> Saying "yes" to fear is telling God that you cannot trust Him to deal with a situation or a problem.

Step 3: Say "no!" to fear. In the Bible, God consistently tells his people one thing when it comes to being afraid: "Stop it!" Three times in the first chapter of Joshua alone, God commanded Joshua not to fear but to be strong and courageous so that Israel might go in and take possession of the Promised Land. Jesus also reminded His followers to "take heart" because He had overcome the world (John 16:33). And the apostle Paul summed up what should be our approach to fear when he wrote, "For God has not given us a spirit of fear, but of power and of love and of a sound mind" (2 Timothy 1:7 NKJV).

Saying "yes" to fear is telling God that you cannot trust Him to deal with a situation or a problem. On the other hand, saying "no" to fear is telling Him that you trust Him and that you're willing to step out, take some risks, and try to accomplish great things so that you can glorify Him.

When it comes to saying "no" to fear, I have to say this: It's worked for me!

Early in our marriage, my wife and I committed ourselves to going anywhere God called us to serve. We decided we would never let fear of unknown places keep us from doing what He wanted us to do. We did not feel called as missionaries in the traditional sense, but more as "tentmakers"—people who, like the apostle Paul with his tentmaking business, used their businesses as a way to finance and support what God had called them to do.

I've learned that I have to be careful what I pray for, because God takes me at my word. Because I've prayerfully committed myself to believing God and to not giving in to fear, I have had the opportunity to travel, work, and/or live in nearly fifty countries on six continents. My wife has also been used in miraculous ways to encourage people and to birth prayer ministries in various parts of the world. We know that God is not yet done with us, but we also know that if we were to allow fear to control us, we would miss out on the great blessings He has in store for us.

When you are faced with a situation—in business or anywhere else—that causes you to feel fear, you have two choices: Give in to the fear, or trust in God and move on. When you choose the latter, when you look your fears in the face and say, "My God is bigger than you," you open the way for opportunities to bless God, to bless others, and to be blessed yourself.

Step 4: Take your best shot. Wayne Gretzky, arguably the greatest player in the history of the National Hockey League, once said, "You miss 100 percent of the shots you never take."

"The Great One" dominated the National Hockey League like no player before him and no player since. He led his teams to four Stanley Cup Championships and finished his career as the holder of virtually every offensive record, including goals, assists, and points. He won ten Art Ross Trophies as the league's leading scorer, nine Hart Trophies as the regular season Most Valuable Player, and two Conn Smythe Trophies as playoff MVP.

Wayne Gretzky's brilliant hockey career is an illustration of what we can do when we refuse to give in to fear, when we look at all obstacles in front of us but are still willing in spite of our fears to "take our best shot."

Over the course of my career, I've been in several situations in which I needed to take my best shot if I was going to succeed. One of the most memorable examples of that was in early 2001, when I began working for Vanguard Airlines.

When I accepted the position as CEO and president of Vanguard, it was with the full understanding that this was a "turnaround" situation, meaning that the airline was asking me to reverse a bad situation. For most of its existence, Vanguard had suffered financially, due mostly to the fact that it lacked a focused business plan and because the airline flew old planes across a confused and ever-changing route structure. Change was needed, and, fortunately, our current majority shareholders were committed to making it.

> If you want to overcome fear, you first need to remember that you are not called to a life of fear.

The turnaround process at Vanguard had begun in early 2001, just before I joined. Upon my arrival, we intensified the effort. We adopted an entirely new—and much better—route structure, leased newer planes with lots of legroom in coach, and initiated a new computer reservation system. We also invested in affordable business-class products and more advanced airline revenue management techniques. Finally, we committed to running on schedule and instilling a positive "can do" attitude in the beleaguered airline staff.

We made considerable progress in the first months of 2001, and Vanguard even began to show small profits the following summer. Finally—in its sixth year of existence—the Vanguard team began to see that the airline could operate successfully.

While the terrorist attacks of September 11, 2001, and their aftermath thwarted what I believe would have been long-term success at Vanguard, I still see our successes earlier that year as an example of what can happen when leaders take their best shot, even in the face of difficult times.

If you want to overcome fear, you first need to remember that you are not called to a life of fear. Then you need to be honest with yourself and with God about your fears. After that, you can say "no" to fear and take your best shot.

But there is a critical ingredient you'll need to add to this mixture, which we discuss in the next chapter.

Principle 2:

REMEMBER TO PRAY

"Therefore I tell you,
whatever you ask for in prayer,
believe that you have received it,
and it will be yours."

Mark 11:24

IT HAS BEEN SAID THAT THERE are no atheists in foxholes, meaning that whether or not someone believes in a God who is active in the affairs of daily human life, he or she will nearly always turn to Him in a time of personal crisis.

I couldn't agree with that assessment more. After all, I've seen it personally—in my life and in the lives of others.

I have always been amazed when I see how eagerly people turn to God during tough times. It seems that when livelihoods are at stake, most people—even those who aren't believers or even necessarily "religious"—tend to look to God for help. The days and weeks following the events of September 11, 2001, were a stark example of this.

On the Friday following the terrorist attacks, President Bush called a frightened and disillusioned America to a National Day of Prayer, and millions gladly took part.

I myself decided to take part in the Day of Prayer and also decided to give the people of Vanguard Airlines an opportunity to join me. I invited our officers and employees—any who could attend and who wanted to attend—to join me that afternoon in one of the larger rooms in our Kansas City headquarters for what I called a corporate prayer meeting.

I had no idea how the people at Vanguard would respond to my invitation. I knew there were some believers in the ranks, but I also knew there were those who had no interest in prayer meetings—at least until today.

As the time for the service neared, staff from every department began pouring into the room. By the time we started the meeting, nearly two hundred people—from custodians to senior officers—were there. It was an incredible turnout considering the fact that we had started resuming flight operations and that many employees were therefore at the airport assisting customers and getting planes ready to fly.

As a team, the people at the prayer meeting spent about thirty minutes interceding for the nation, for those who lost loved ones in the attacks, for our colleagues directly affected by the catastrophe, and for our own airline.

Time and time again, we saw God provide for us.

That prayer meeting was not the end of our seeking God over our future, either. Over the coming months, prayer became an increasingly important part of many Vanguard employees' lives. New crises, which seemed to arrive almost daily, called for more prayer, and many responded. We did not have another big prayer gathering like the one on

Friday, September 14, but employees continued to pray individually and in small groups, and some mobilized "prayer chains" at their churches.

To this day, I believe that those prayers were honored.

Time and time again, we saw God provide for us. He gave us fresh ideas to raise cash or cut expenses, and we enjoyed times when sales or cash flow improved, sometimes out of proportion with our efforts. Sometimes, bills that had come due slipped to a later date at the vendor's doing, when cash flow was better.

I saw up close and personal the power of prayer in the face of tough times. It was a time when God taught me new things about prayer and a time when He confirmed the lessons I'd already learned.

Later in this chapter, we're going to take a look at some of the ways we can cover our businesses in prayer, particularly during difficult times. But before we do that, let's examine the components I've learned to turn into effective prayer.

THE INGREDIENTS OF EFFECTIVE PRAYER

I have to admit that going to God in prayer during the tough times is not something I do naturally. My training and professional background as an analyst naturally make me something of a "worst-case scenario" kind of person. That's sound thinking when it comes to analyzing and fixing problems in the world of business, specifically in the world of transportation, but it's not so sound when it comes to matters of faith. But God, using my precious wife, Priscilla, other people, and my own experiences, has taught me over the years that there is no better approach than to take my worries and concerns directly to Him.

But that's not all He's taught me. He has also given me what you might call a format for my prayers. No, it's not the recitation of a mantra or prayer; rather, it's a formula I've found in the pages of the Bible. It is what some have called the "ACTS" format, ACTS being an acronym for different parts of an effective prayer life.

Here is what that kind of praying looks like:

1. *Adoration and praise*: Nothing draws us closer to the Lord than speaking words to Him of adoration and praise. No, God doesn't need us to praise Him; He knows full well who He is and what He can do. Rather, He wants us to express our love for Him this way because that is what He created us to do.

When God created the very first human beings, He did so because He wanted to have fellowship with beings who were, in many ways, just like Him. He wanted to have a real relationship with beings He could love and communicate with and who could respond to Him likewise.

There is indeed great power in speaking praises to God. When we do so, we in effect acknowledge that He is able to overcome even our worst difficulties and see us through tough times and that He is above any and all life circumstances. For that reason, whether or not we like the circumstances we're in, we need to verbally proclaim that God is in control over everything, including our problems and struggles.

King David, who endured his share of difficult times, wrote these words of praise:

> *Don't worry about the wicked. Don't envy those who do wrong. For like grass, they soon fade away. Like springtime flowers, they soon wither. Trust in the LORD and do good. Then you will live safely in the land and prosper. Take delight in the LORD, and he will give you your heart's desires.*
>
> PSALM 37:1–4 NLT

David was obviously facing some serious injustices when he wrote this psalm. David tried to do good, but his efforts seemed to be failing him. Meanwhile, the wicked were prospering. Yet David didn't lose perspective. On the contrary, he remembered to keep his focus on God and God alone and offer Him words of praise.

When we praise God, especially in the midst of tough times, we not only invite Him to pick us up and calm our hearts and remind us that He is in control, but we also invite Him to step in and make a tangible difference in our situations.

2. *Confession of sin*: The Bible tells us, "The prayer of a righteous man is powerful and effective" (James 5:16). In other

words, when we are right with God, He hears us and responds to our prayers. And how are we made right with God? Through the confession of our sins. The apostle John summed this up perfectly when he wrote, "If we confess our sins, he is faithful and just and will forgive us our sins and purify us from all unrighteousness" (1 John 1:9).

I believe that no time of prayer can be complete unless it includes a time of confession—for the smallest sins all the way up to what we consider the "biggies."

3. *Thanksgiving*: The apostle Paul offers us these instructions when it comes to prayer: "Do not be anxious about anything, but in everything, by prayer and petition, with thanksgiving, present your requests to God" (Philippians 4:6). The two key words in this verse are "with thanksgiving," meaning that if we want God to hear and respond to our prayers, we need to thank Him for who He is and what He's done for us.

This can be especially hard to do when times are tough. But the Bible gives us an example of what thanksgiving in the time of crisis looks like: "Though the fig tree does not bud and there are no grapes on the vines, though the olive crop fails and the fields produce no food, though there are no sheep in the pen and no cattle in the stalls, yet I will rejoice in the LORD, I will be joyful in God my Savior" (Habakkuk 3:17–18).

4. *Supplication*: This is a fancy, biblical-sounding word that

simply means prayerfully taking our specific requests to the Lord. It's also something that Paul says to do in Philippians 4:6!

A lot of us, depending on our backgrounds, wonder if God wants to hear our specific requests. But the Bible assures us over and over that God is willing and able to meet all our needs if we but ask.

Think of it this way: If you as a father or mother had a son who needed something—anything from a new pair of shoes to money to pay for college tuition to a life-saving surgery—you would dip as far into your resources as possible to meet that need. What's more, you'd do it gladly, simply out of your love for your child. But our heavenly Father is a God who loves us beyond anything even we as parents can comprehend. This is part of what Jesus was talking about when He said, "Look at the birds of the air; they do not sow or reap or store away in barns, and yet your heavenly Father feeds them. Are you not much more valuable than they?" (Matthew 6:26).

I have always been fascinated by this call to ceaseless prayer, and for many years I wondered how could I do it in the workplace and still get my job done.

But there's more to this. You see, God's resources, unlike ours, are infinitely unlimited. That's why Paul wrote later on in the book of Philippians, "And my God will meet all your needs according to his glorious riches in Christ Jesus" (4:19).

This is the kind of prayer that honors God, and it's the kind of prayer we as leaders should practice in every situation, no matter how easy or difficult it is. And it's the kind of prayer the Bible tells us should be an ongoing and growing part of our lives.

PRAYING WITHOUT CEASING

Paul gave us some very important instructions on prayer when he wrote, "Pray without ceasing" (1 Thessalonians 5:17 NKJV). I have always been fascinated by this call to ceaseless prayer, and for many years I wondered how could I do it in the workplace and still get my job done.

As I've thought about it, I have come to realize that our God is always the very essence of practicality. Because of that, I've recognized that there are many ways to "pray without ceasing." It's simply a matter of being creative. It might mean whispering one-line prayers the moment a situation arises, praying while commuting to and from the office, or uttering a quick prayer at work while shuffling paper or becoming immersed in a project.

I've also come to believe that "praying without ceasing"—particularly in the business world—can mean building a sort of "prayer network," starting with leading the willing in group prayer at the office.

THE POWER OF GROUP PRAYER

My experience with group prayer at Vanguard Airlines wasn't

my first in that area in my business life. Over the course of my career, I have had many opportunities to help introduce group prayer into companies I have worked for—as a midlevel analyst, as a senior executive, and as a CEO. I have started prayer groups in different corporate and national cultures, and I have found that they can work no matter where you work, what cultural setting you are in, or what position you hold in your company.

My first experience in forming a prayer group at work came shortly after my arrival as a midlevel analyst at what I thought would be my "dream job."

In late 1989, I finally realized a lifelong dream of working in the airline industry. Flying had always fascinated me, and I wanted to work for an airline. My father, the pastor of a growing Presbyterian church in Minneapolis during my years growing up, fueled my interest in aviation, as he had served as a gunner on a B-29 bomber near the end of World War II. As I was growing up, air transportation just seemed to be in my blood. I read voraciously about all aspects of aviation and studied airline route maps and schedules every chance I got.

I wanted to be a pilot, but unfortunately, I grew up in an era when the qualifications for pilots included perfect, uncorrected vision. I did not qualify in that area, so over time I moved into the administrative arena.

Eventually, I found myself working as an analyst in the planning department of American Airlines, one of the world's biggest carriers. It didn't take me long to see how volatile the airline industry could be. A little over a year after I started my newfound career, the industry faced a major downturn stemming from the first Persian Gulf War. Passenger traffic and revenue declined significantly, and many airlines posted billion-dollar losses. "Downsizing"—in other words, laying off people—became the order of the day at all major U.S.-based airlines, and several rounds of layoffs decimated the numbers at American. As you might have guessed, the people at American were caught up in fear, stress, and worry.

Times were tough, so I and several other Christians in my department began meeting weekly to pray through the crisis. The group, composed of believers of all denominational stripes, formed when several people simultaneously recognized the need for prayer inside the corporation. At least once a week, three to ten people met around noon in a small conference room.

Our efforts touched everyone in the group—spiritually as well as professionally. People grew in their faith, and God did great things in some of their personal lives. No, we did not all avoid layoffs. Some of the prayer group members were eventually let go. Nonetheless, God took care of them, and they found alternative, and sometimes better, employment.

GROUP PRAYER IN A LATIN LOCALE

Ten years after my initial employment in the airline industry, I accepted a position as an executive at Grupo TACA, one of the larger airlines in Latin America. It was then that I took up residence in El Salvador, which was home to the airline's headquarters.

Our airline faced many crises, some of which were results of intense competition from the large, deep-pocketed U.S. airlines that were trying—rather successfully—to move in on the Central American market in a major way. Naturally, our airline struggled in the face of the competition.

I and some other believers in the company had started a prayer group, and during the lean financial months of late 1998, our prayer group lifted up the company's need for revenue growth. Over the next few business quarters, while other airlines struggled to produce any revenue growth in the Central American market, our revenue grew at double the normal rate. To us, it was clearly an answer to prayer.

Workplace Prayer: It Can Work for You

My personal experiences with prayer in the workplace have made me a big advocate of starting prayer groups in the workplace. Because of that, I've enjoyed God's blessings during even the most difficult of times.

Do you want to see God's power at work in your life, especially during "down" times? Then find someone to pray with at work—maybe even several "someones."

But how do we start effective prayer groups at work? How do we do that without alienating others or creating divisions within the workforce? Let me suggest a few guidelines—guidelines I've tried and found to be very helpful.

KNOW WHAT GROUP PRAYER IS AND ISN'T

I want to start this section by saying that when we engage in group prayer or when we mobilize a broad base of prayer support, we are not playing a numbers game with God, and we are not "twisting His arm" in an attempt to get Him to act as we see fit. That wouldn't work anyway!

On the contrary, when we gather together to pray—be it in a church, in a home, in an office, or anywhere else people can assemble—we are gathering together both to honor God and to draw close to one another.

Jesus encouraged us to do just that when He told His disciples, "For where two or three have gathered together in My name, I am there in their midst" (Matthew 18:20 NASB). This strongly suggests that God not only allows for group prayer, but He actually *encourages* it!

Prayer is worship, and worship honors and blesses God. Therefore, when we have many praying with and for us, God is worshiped and glorified all the more. God speaks to us—through scripture, through that "still small voice," and through wise counsel from godly people, just to name a few avenues—and blesses us when we worship Him. That is what the psalmist meant when he wrote, "God presides in the great assembly" (Psalm 82:1).

The book of Acts, which tells the story of the birth and growth of the early church, contains this account of the activities of one particular fellowship of believers: "They devoted themselves to the apostles' teaching and to the fellowship, to the breaking of bread *and to prayer*" (Acts 2:42, italics mine). This gathering of saints was part of God's plan to bring unity within the body of Christ, which they would most certainly need as they faced opposition from the outside world.

So feel encouraged to gather in prayer! It pleases God, and it draws you closer to your brothers and sisters in Christ.

USE WISDOM

Starting a prayer group in your place of work isn't a matter of simply calling people together to pray. No, we as leaders must use wisdom when we start these kinds of groups. In the words of Jesus, we must be "as cunning as a snake, inoffensive as a dove" (Matthew 10:16 MSG) when we make prayer groups a part of our company's business culture.

> Make sure that people understand that attendance at the prayer groups is completely *optional*.

Here are some wise steps you can take in starting your prayer group:

1. *Open the prayer group to everyone, and make sure they know that it is optional.* When you send out invitations to a prayer meeting

at your company, make sure you open it to *everyone*—from the custodians and clerks to the upper-level corporate leadership. Also (and this is absolutely essential), make sure that people understand that attendance at the prayer groups is completely *optional*. That way, you avoid all appearances of coercion, thus avoiding all sorts of conflicts that could come if someone believes they are required to engage in activities they may not personally believe in.

2. *Be careful how and what you share about company needs to a broader group of employees.* Some issues may not be "shareable" due to corporate confidentiality requirements, so you must be careful what kind of prayer requests you make at the prayer meetings. When in doubt, either take the matter as an individual prayer assignment (between you and God) or share your prayer requests only with those who are "cleared" to have the information contained in the request.

3. *Be respectful of the spiritual backgrounds represented in the group.* When you start a corporate prayer group, you want to create an atmosphere in which a broad segment of the employees feel both comfortable and welcome to attend. So take the time to find out what kind of sensibilities and sensitivities might be represented within your prayer group. By that I mean find out if some members might be offended by practices such as, for example, praying in tongues. If some members are uncomfortable with this practice, do not use it in your

prayer group. Remember, you are not forming a prayer group just to push a particular denominational agenda but to glorify God and lift up the needs of your fellow employees and the company.

4. *Keep everything prayed about in the group in strict confidence.* Do not gossip. Make sure that what is talked about in the prayer group stays in the prayer group. That includes personal as well as corporate concerns that come up.

5. *Meet at times that do not disrupt company work flow, and be punctual.* It's not advisable or appropriate to allow your prayer group meetings to cut into company time. Use lunch times or break times or meet before or after work. Begin and end at a set time, and always do so within the time the company allots. Do not be late for work.

One final note on starting a prayer group at work: If you are an entry or midlevel employee wishing to start a prayer group at your place of work, make sure you get permission to do so from someone who has the authority to give it. If your employer will not permit prayer on the job, respect that decision—even if you feel it is unjust. As an alternative, take the prayer time off-site. Meet in a nearby church, restaurant, park, parking lot, or in someone's home (of course, the list goes on) before or after work. Also, make sure you let your superiors know you are praying for the company. More often than not, they will appreciate it, even if they are not believers.

Be Organized

It is vital that a prayer group follow some kind of order or format. Otherwise, people will end up wasting time without getting much praying done.

Here are a few tips for effective prayer in a group setting:

1. *Set and keep a time for prayer*. I have been involved with many prayer groups, and I have found that thirty minutes is the optimal time to do some serious praying and still cater to the needs and experiences of the group. The majority of the people in your company will probably find spending more than thirty minutes in prayer a great challenge—especially during the workday.

2. *Appoint a leader*. Every prayer group needs someone to take charge and lead. This is the person who convenes the group, sets a format, and makes sure that the prayer time is focused and timely.

3. *Use some kind of structure*. Each group will take on a structure of its own. One good and simple format is to open with a short scripture reading, followed by a word of encouragement based on that reading, followed by the sharing of prayer requests, followed, of course, by the actual praying.

4. *Pray according to scripture*. God gives us literally hundreds of promises in scripture, many of which relate to business situations. Therefore, it's a good idea to incorporate these promises

into your prayer time by praying them to God in His own words as recorded in the Bible. Praying scripture back to God is powerful as it shows Him that you care enough about Him to commit His words to memory. Jesus did this very kind of praying as the devil tried to tempt Him. Each of Jesus' rebukes to Satan was based on passages from the Old Testament (see Matthew 4:1–11).

Now let's take a look at some other kinds of prayer for your position in life.

"OUTSIDE" PRAYER RESOURCES

I have learned that in addition to the people within companies or businesses who are willing to join their leaders in prayer, there are an endless number of "human resources"—individuals and organizations—who are willing to help us keep our businesses covered in prayer.

> I often asked the pastors and elders to pray for various concerns at our airline, and they enthusiastically complied.

Let's consider some of those resources.

THE LOCAL CHURCH AND "PARACHURCH" ORGANIZATIONS

At the beginning of the twenty-first century, many churches and "parachurch" organizations are beginning to recognize that businesses are an extension of their ministries and are therefore committing themselves to praying for businesses and business leaders. That only makes sense, as fully employed people spend upwards of 25 percent of their time each week at work, with many spending a far greater proportion of their time in work-related pursuits.

Over the course of my career as a business leader, God has led me to mobilize these kinds of organizations to pray for my company—for its leadership, employees, stockholders, and customers alike.

For example, my home church in Dallas has a ministry and prayer time devoted exclusively to the marketplace and also hosts a monthly small group for Christian CEOs, business owners, and executives. Over the years, I have found these ministries to be very important resources as I sought out "outside" prayer for the companies I worked for.

Also, during my time in El Salvador, I attended a local church—*Iglesia Cristo a Las Naciones* (Christ to the Nations Church)—whose members prayed for every dimension of life, including that of business. They prayed passionately because unemployment was high, and keeping businesses alive and healthy was vital to the nation. I often asked the pastors and elders to pray for various concerns at our airline, and they enthusiastically complied.

Finally, when I began working for Vanguard Airlines, I immediately sought out Kansas City–area churches and parachurch organizations and asked them to pray for the airline. Almost all of them were happy to oblige.

PEER GROUP SUPPORT

Many circumstances in the business world preclude the sharing of a prayer need in a group setting. In a situation like that, you need a group of Christian peers in whom you can confide. But how do you find a peer group? Start by looking at your local church for a group of peers—meaning fellow business leaders—outside your particular business and, preferably, outside your particular industry.

I found peer support by connecting with local churches almost as soon as I arrived at Vanguard. The pastors knew the mature Christian business leaders in their congregations and throughout Kansas City. We arranged a series of meetings, and soon I had about a half-dozen godly businesspeople to whom I could turn for support and prayer when things got rough.

"INTERNATIONALIZING" PRAYER

Over the years, Priscilla and I have had the opportunity to travel to countries on every continent except Antarctica—both for business and for ministry. These travels have allowed us to build up a global network of Christian contacts—from places such as India, Sri Lanka, Great Britain, Germany, El Salvador, Guatemala, Mexico, and Honduras—with whom we could share prayer requests.

> It is dangerous work, as militant Hindus have beaten him and his colleagues on several occasions.

One of these many contacts is a man I'll call "Pastor J." (I refer to him this way because the area in which he serves in India is the site of persecution of Christians.) Pastor J. is a small man with a big heart for God. He and his team plant churches in some "unreached" portions of India. It is dangerous work, as militant Hindus have beaten him and his colleagues on several occasions.

In the aftermath of September 11, I included Pastor J. on my e-mail list whenever Vanguard Airlines had a specific need. He always wrote back, assuring me that he, his family, and his congregation were praying for Vanguard. Between twenty-five and fifty men and women—mostly unemployed gold field workers, most of whom had probably never even seen an airplane—attended Pastor J.'s church, and they prayed regularly for Vanguard.

Prayer support of this type is a two-way street. I knew that Pastor J. had more dire issues confronting him than I faced at Vanguard. Because of that, I always took time to discover his needs and remember them in prayer.

FAMILY PRAYER SUPPORT

If you remember one thing from this chapter—other than the need to go to God and pray over business specifics—remember to pray with your spouse and family.

If your spouse is a Christian, you have someone with whom you can share your burdens and a wonderful intercessor who knows you and your needs intimately. If you are not married—single, divorced, or widowed—then you can look to your parents, your extended family, or your children for prayer and support.

I have been multiply blessed when it comes to family prayer support. My wife, our sons, my parents, and my sister are all people to whom I can turn for prayer support, especially when I am facing a trial or crisis.

My wife is God's greatest earthly gift to me. Priscilla is an intercessor who has incredible insight into God's truths, into scripture, and into different kinds of situations. She is not a businessperson, and she does not understand all the ins and outs of the airline industry (although she probably has learned more about airlines and transportation than she ever imagined she would when we first married), but she doesn't need to in order to be my support.

Next, let's take a look at the most important kind of prayer you can do: one-on-one, between you and God.

YOU AND GOD ALONE

In an environment in which business scandals make international news, there are times when you as a Christian business leader must be very careful not to divulge your company's needs or issues to any "outsiders." Laws and regulations govern much of our behavior as executives, and many business agreements contain written confidentiality or nondisclosure clauses. If you serve in a "public" company—one governed by Security and Exchange Commission (SEC) regulations—you must be all the more guarded about what you say, as well as to whom and when you say it.

That was my situation at Vanguard, which, at the time I took over as CEO and president, was heavily indebted to vendors who could have legally shut us down at any time. Vanguard was a publicly traded company, and I and the other officers of the airline had to be extremely careful what we said and to whom. For that reason, I needed to word my prayer requests concerning Vanguard's situation very carefully. I had to keep the details as to what we owed and to whom to myself.

But Vanguard did not survive, and for weeks before and after the shutdown, it troubled me that it appeared that God did not keep His promises.

In cases like the one I endured at Vanguard, we as business leaders have only one place to go with many of our prayer requests: to God Himself. Yes, we can ask our prayer groups and "outside" intercessors to pray for God's favor on our companies and to pray that He will bless our relationships with vendors, stockholders, and others. But when it comes to the sensitive details, we must wait until we are alone with our most trusted Business Advisor: our heavenly Father.

A FINAL WORD OF CAUTION

As you and your intercessors faithfully pray for your struggling business, you and those prayer partners may feel that God is telling you that your company or corporation will survive or prosper. Near the end of Vanguard's existence, I and many of our intercessors—people I trusted as those who had deep, abiding relationships with the Lord—firmly believed that Vanguard would keep flying.

But Vanguard did not survive, and for weeks before and after the shutdown, it troubled me that it appeared that God did not keep His promises. I had a personal crisis of faith, and I wondered if God had failed us, and I wondered if I had somehow "blown it" and was reaping the consequences.

During those painful weeks after Vanguard's shutdown, Priscilla and I talked and prayed over these issues, and it became clear that God had not failed us and that I had not "blown it." I realized that my staff and I had done everything in our power to save Vanguard—including praying faithfully—but that it was simply beyond saving. And it became clear that God was not finished with us or with the others at Vanguard.

This time in my life was a reminder to me that God's ways are not our ways and that His timing is not our timing. To this day, I believe God will keep His promises to us—in His own way and in His own timing.

If you are going through tough times as a business leader right now, don't forget to pray and to ask others to pray for and with you. Then wait and watch what unfolds as God moves. He may not move in exactly the way you had hoped for and expected, but He will most certainly move. And He'll do it in a way that glorifies Him and in a way that is best for you.

PRINCIPLE 3:

GET GOD'S PERSPECTIVE

But I have stilled and quieted my soul;
like a weaned child with its mother,
like a weaned child is my soul within me.

PSALM 131:2

WHEN I FIRST BECAME CHAIR-
man and CEO of Vanguard Airlines, I knew I had a lot of
hard work to do if the airline was to overcome its history as a
financial "loser." Everyone in the industry knew that Vanguard was in dire straits, mostly because it had languished
under the "business plan of the month" style of management
used by a series of CEOs and majority shareholders.

I knew going in that the only way to bring positive, last-
ing change to Vanguard was to introduce some badly needed
stability into its management and operations, and from the
day I arrived there, that's exactly what I sought to do.

From the very beginning, it was taxing work. I spent long,
hard hours making the changes I knew needed to be made if
Vanguard was to survive and prosper in the competitive world
of the airline industry. But during those first few months at
Vanguard, as I poured myself into making it a successful airline,
I had no idea what kind of anguish and stress lay ahead for me.

Just as I started to see the fruit of my labors at Vanguard—as I pointed out earlier, by the summer of 2001, this perpetual loser actually started turning some modest profits—I was confronted with the sometimes incredible stress of operating an airline in the post–September 11 environment.

> To some degree, leaders thrive on the endless tasks and intensity that almost every day brings.

In the coming months, as I tried to run an airline struggling to survive in a world turned upside down by one of the most horrific acts of terror in history, I found that I really needed to hear from God. In other words, I needed to take the time to get some perspective—His perspective.

That's when I found it absolutely essential, particularly for my own peace of mind, to get away and meet with God in what I call "quiet places."

Finding Perspective in the Quiet Places

Leaders don't get much in the way of "quiet time," particularly when their businesses are going through tough times. They must come up with strategic and tactical plans, so they must be visionaries. They must understand their businesses, their customers, and the environment in which they work, so they need to remain "in the loop" when it comes to the day-to-day operations of their company. To some degree, leaders thrive on the endless tasks and intensity that almost every day brings. They flourish in an atmosphere in which they have to handle endless phone calls, negotiations, planning sessions, one-on-one meetings with key staff, and e-mails.

But godly leaders, no matter how busy they are and no matter how many tasks they must undertake, need to seek out God and get His perspective.

But how do we do that? Can we get God's perspective while playing golf? Perhaps. What about when we are boating or walking? Sometimes. By going fishing? Well, according to my friends who enjoy fishing, their times on a river or out on a lake can be some times of their closest fellowship with God.

But can we really discern *all* God has for us while we are out resting and recreating? I don't think so.

I believe it is important for the business leader to get away and take part in some rest and recreation by engaging in activities he or she enjoys. I also believe that God can speak in many different ways and in many different situations. In fact, I as a business leader have received inspiration in a wide variety of circumstances, including recreational ones. But I have come to believe that if we are truly committed to leading in a way that pleases God, we need to give Him some undivided attention.

That means taking time to get away to quiet places where we can encounter God personally and intimately. That's important even in the best of times, but it's absolutely essential during difficult or stressful times.

Would you like an example of the importance of taking the time to get perspective? Look no further than Jesus Christ Himself.

FINDING A QUIET PLACE: OUR EXAMPLE

Jesus carried infinitely more responsibility than anyone else in human history. While the decisions of leaders of even the largest corporations may affect the lives of thousands, maybe even millions, Jesus' decisions would affect the eternities of literally billions—everyone who has lived, lives now, or will live in the future.

> But instead of trying to "go alone," He prepared Himself for what was ahead by going to a quiet place so He could be alone with the Father.

During His earthly ministry, Jesus led an incredibly full life of teaching, preaching, healing, and performing miracles. While Jesus was God in the flesh, He was also very much human, and there were times when He left His teaching, healing, and miracle working behind to spend time alone with His Father. It was during those times that His spirit was renewed. It was also during those times that He got direction from above—when He got the Father's perspective.

The Gospel of Mark reports how near the beginning of Jesus' earthly ministry, after a very long day of performing miracles of healing, He spent some time with the Father in a quiet place: "Very early in the morning, while it was still dark, Jesus got up, left the house and went off to a solitary place, where he prayed" (Mark 1:35).

Later on, when Jesus' work on earth was nearly complete, He was in absolute agony over what was before Him, namely His arrest, trial, and crucifixion. But instead of trying to "go it alone," He prepared Himself for what was ahead by going to a quiet place so He could be alone with the Father. In Matthew 26, we see a wrenching, amazing account of how time alone with the Father gave Jesus the perspective He needed to finish the mission for which He had come to earth in the first place. In the quiet of the Garden of Gethsemane and with a heart filled with sorrow, Jesus prayed, "My Father, if it is possible, may this cup be taken from me. Yet not as I will, but as you will" (Matthew 26:39).

Jesus modeled perfectly how we should live our lives, and that includes in our ministries, businesses, and relationships. And if Jesus, who was in complete control of every aspect of His earthly life, needed to get away to quiet places, then we as mere human leaders—people who are only partly in control of only a limited part of our lives—need all the more to do the same.

But in the midst of busy, stressful lives, how can we find the time to get away to a quiet place? Furthermore, how can we find such places? Let's examine this concept.

FINDING THE QUIET PLACES

It's not always easy for many business leaders to find the quiet places, let alone the time to spend in them. But believe me, it *can* be done!

The first step in spending time with God in the quiet places is a relatively simple one. It's simply finding a place where you can spend some uninterrupted time with Him. These places aren't hard to find. In fact, the quiet places are all around us, even for those of us who live in the biggest, busiest cities. All we have to do is look!

Most any city, suburb, or rural area has places where you can find quiet—parks, seasides, and waterfronts, for example. And if you can't find a place outside your own world, try looking closer. Your own home may include a quiet office, a peaceful spot in the backyard, or any number of places you can get away from everything. And, when worse comes to worst, you can take the time to simply ask God to show you a good quiet place to meet with Him.

When I was living and working in El Salvador, I found a couple such quiet places. One was a park just a couple blocks from my apartment that overlooked the city of San Salvador from its perch on the side of a mountain. It was a great place to get away from everything and just walk and pray. I also made use of the balcony of my apartment, which sat on the side of a volcano that had not erupted for decades. I could see almost the entire city from that spot, including the home of the owner of the airline I worked for.

When I moved to Kansas City to begin working for Vanguard Airlines, I found a wonderful quiet place, and during those times of stress and despair—and there were many of them in those days—I made regular use of that place. Believe it or not, it was located in nearby Leavenworth. Yes, the same Leavenworth that is home to the famous, or infamous, federal penitentiary!

I have always been something of a history and geography buff, and living in Kansas City afforded me the opportunity to do some "exploring" of historic sites. Leavenworth sat at a point that Lewis and Clark passed on their great voyage to open the American West. It was here in the 1800s that thousands of pioneers in wagons began their arduous journeys from the eastern United States to the unknown bastions of the American West. From this location, railroads also began to penetrate the West.

> The sound of the gentle rushing of the water and the wind rustling the leaves of the great trees offered a wonderful change of pace from the hectic activity at the office.

As I explored some of these historic sites, I discovered a peaceful and beautiful park in Leavenworth, one that was seldom used in the evenings. I found a nice bench at the north end of the park just a few feet from the river. This quiet place was shaded by great elm and cottonwood trees. The sound of the gentle rushing of the water and the wind rustling the leaves of the great trees offered a wonderful change of pace from the hectic activity at the office. Foxes, squirrels, and raccoons wandered through the park, and river birds darted above the water looking for insects. Deer frequently trotted down to the riverside to drink in the cool of the evening, while a couple of beavers worked on their lodge in a quiet inlet on the opposite bank.

At that time in my career, I often needed a change of pace, and this was it. And the most beautiful part of this place was that, more often than not, I had it all to myself!

After a hard, intense day of activity at the Vanguard corporate office, it was always a blessing to go to that quiet place to unwind. I cannot count the number of evenings I spent in that park after work pouring out my heart to God, worshipping Him, and getting His perspective.

COMMUNICATING WITH GOD IN THE QUIET PLACES

I hadn't been coming to my quiet place in Leavenworth long before I developed something of a format for communicating with God in a quiet place. It's a format I've used ever since and one I believe can be helpful for anyone who wants to meet with God in a quiet place.

Here's what it looks like:

1. *Start by praising God.* One of the most important lessons I've learned over the course of my career is that attitude means everything. I've also learned that my attitude must be

one that inspires me to praise God—especially during difficult times. I've learned to follow the leading of the apostle Paul, a man who endured more than his share of difficult times, who wrote, "Rejoice in the Lord always. I will say it again: Rejoice!" (Philippians 4:4).

In chapter 3, I pointed out that there is great power in praise. Praise literally brings us into the presence of God, and that's a very soothing place to be during times of stress and uncertainty.

When I go to my quiet places to be with the Lord, I start by spending time just speaking words of praise. I encourage you to do the same. Praise God when things are going well and when they're not going so well. Praise God when it makes no human sense to do so! When you do that, you open up lines of communication to the Lord, which will bring you to the second part of your time with Him in your quiet place.

2. *Talk to God honestly about the distress you are feeling over your circumstances.* This is difficult for a lot of business leaders, many of whom are "wired" to keep certain things to themselves. It can be especially difficult for those of us who don't understand that God actually wants us to talk to Him about our struggles. *Does God really want to hear about my problems?* we wonder to ourselves.

Indeed He does! The Bible contains many examples of godly people who brought their problems before God. King David, for example, spoke these honestly painful words to his

Lord: "Listen to my prayer, O God, do not ignore my plea; hear me and answer me. My thoughts trouble me and I am distraught" (Psalm 55:1–2).

When things were at their worst at Vanguard, I used part of my time in my quiet place to speak to God of the distress in my heart over that particular day's events. I talked to Him about large bills that were due, about our need for a boost in revenue, about how we were struggling to find new investment dollars for Vanguard. I also often talked with Him about the events in Washington, D.C., where the United States Congress had passed legislation to provide financial assistance to struggling airlines, none of which would be coming to Vanguard.

I wasn't grumbling or complaining, either. Rather, I was honestly sharing with my God the things that had me so stressed and anguished. I knew then and know now what we all need to lay hold of when it comes to taking our problems to God: He can handle it!

How important do you think it is to God that you listen for His voice?

3. *Be quiet and listen.* When you make an effort to spend time with God in a quiet place, it's important that after you praise Him and pray about your circumstances, you take time to just listen. Unfortunately, too many godly leaders spend all their time with God talking to Him but don't take time to just listen.

How important do you think it is to God that you listen for His voice? Consider these words from scripture: "Now choose life, so that you and your children may live and that you may love the LORD your God, *listen to his voice*, and hold fast to him. For the LORD is your life, and he will give you many years in the land he swore to give to your fathers, Abraham, Isaac and Jacob" (Deuteronomy 30:19–20, italics added).

When I go to my quiet places to meet with God, after I spend time praising Him and talking to Him about what is going on in my life, I simply shut up and listen for what the Bible calls the "still small voice" (1 Kings 19:12 NKJV). Most of the time, I don't hear anything, so I just spend time enjoying a sense of God's presence, which brings me peace even in times of turmoil. At other times, however, I sense His leading to take a certain action.

Hearing God is always important, and it's all the more so when you are seeking His comfort and direction during tough times. When we take our concerns and worries to our number one Business Advisor, we get His perspective on every situation we as leaders face.

> We leaders often expect God to meet us where we are, mostly because we are busy and have little time to get away.

And, in many cases, that's when God makes an appointment with us to leave our situations behind and meet with Him. . .at the top of a mountain!

FROM THE QUIET PLACES TO THE MOUNTAINTOPS

Meeting alone with God in a quiet place for prayer and praise is essential for the businessperson of God. But equally vital is being willing to meet God in a time and place He appoints. I have learned that if I want God's perspective on things, I need to pay attention to my surroundings and to those calls to climb to the "mountaintops" where I can experience Him in a more profound way.

Mountaintops are significant places in scripture. They symbolize an effort on the part of humankind to move closer to God. Reaching the top of a mountain is not convenient or easy. Any mountain climber will tell you that it takes tremendous effort to reach the top of a mountain.

At the very least, reaching a summit and meeting with God means going out of our way. We leaders often expect God to meet us where we are, mostly because we are busy and have little time to get away. I believe that God will often take the time to meet in our own little worlds, but I also believe that our most significant and life-changing encounters with Him happen when we go out of our way and make special effort to meet with Him.

DIFFERENT KINDS OF MOUNTAINTOPS

In the Bible, mountaintops were places where God held very special meetings with His people, places where He tested them, communicated with them, and showed them magnificent things about Himself.

Here are some examples, straight from the pages of scripture:

MOUNTAINTOPS OF TESTING

The first mountaintop experience recorded in scripture is found in Genesis 22, where we read of Abraham's testing on a mountain in a place called Moriah. God had called Abraham to do something very curious, namely, sacrifice his only son, Isaac, on an altar. No doubt, Abraham must have wondered what God had in mind. Sacrifice his only son? The son God had promised, then miraculously given him? It just didn't make sense!

But what Abraham didn't know and couldn't have known was that this was a test, one that would show God and Abraham himself that he wasn't going to hold back *anything* from the Lord, not even his very own son.

Abraham, who was no doubt confused and heartbroken over these new marching orders, didn't argue. He was determined to obey his God, even though what he had been told to do seemed, at least in his limited thinking, crazy. He faithfully obeyed in loading his donkey with firewood early the next morning and setting out for Moriah. And he obeyed right up to the "moment of truth." With the fire for the burnt offering blazing before him, Abraham tied up his son and prepared to sacrifice him.

Only then was the test complete. As Abraham raised the knife to finish the act, an angel called out and told him not to kill Isaac, that the Lord would provide another sacrifice that day. Furthermore, the angel delivered this blessed message:

> *"I swear by myself, declares the LORD, that because you have done this and have not withheld your son, your only son, I will surely bless you and make your descendants as numerous as the stars in the sky and as the sand on the seashore. Your descendants will take possession of the cities of their enemies, and through your offspring all nations on earth will be blessed, because you have obeyed me."*

GENESIS 22:16–18

Through this one act of obedience, Abraham received tremendous blessings, blessings that would be carried through history on to millions of God's people. And he also proved himself worthy to be the father of the nation through whom God would bring into the world our Savior, Jesus Christ.

Usually, we believers tend to think of mountaintops as times when we are "flying high" with God, as times when we are basking in His blessings. But the truth of the matter is that mountaintops aren't always a pleasant place to be; in fact, they are often places where our faith *in* God, as well as our faithfulness *to* Him, are tested.

When we are in a time of testing, it's often easy to complain or to look at God and ask, "Why me, Lord?" Just as Abraham probably didn't understand what God was doing when He asked him to sacrifice his son, we don't understand why God is allowing—maybe even causing—us to go through the tests we're enduring.

But when God takes us to a mountaintop of testing, our response shouldn't be to complain but to ask Him to continue showing us what He wants us to learn from our tests. Our response shouldn't be to wonder if God knows what He's doing but to rest in the fact that He knows what is best for us. In fact, when we are faced with these kinds of tests, we should take to heart the words of the apostle James: "Consider it pure joy, my brothers, whenever you face trials of many kinds, because you know that the testing of your faith develops perseverance. Perseverance must finish its work so that you may be mature and complete, not lacking anything" (James 1:2–4).

MOUNTAINTOPS OF COMMUNICATION WITH GOD

Three months after the exodus of the Israelites from Egypt, God had some serious business to discuss with Moses, the man He had called to lead them out of captivity. And where was that meeting to take place? At the top of a mountain!

The Bible tells us, "The LORD descended to the top of Mount Sinai and called Moses to the top of the mountain" (Exodus 19:20). It was there that God made His covenant with the people of Israel, there that He gave Moses the law by which the people were to live, there that God spoke personally to Moses, "as a man speaks with his friend" (Exodus 33:11).

It's an understatement to say that this experience had a profound effect on Moses. Exodus 34:29 tells us that when Moses came down from the mountain, "he was not aware that his face was radiant because he had spoken with the LORD."

Nothing changes us like hearing from the Lord, particularly when we are going through difficult times. And when God invites us to a mountaintop, we should do two things: obey and climb the mountain and listen carefully to Him.

MOUNTAINTOPS OF THE SPECTACULAR

Moses witnessed some spectacular things as he met with God on a mountaintop. In fact, the Bible tells us that he was one of the few people who actually got a glimpse of God's true glory. But the New Testament also tells the story of godly leaders going to a mountaintop and seeing the spectacular.

In the Gospel of Luke, we read the account of what is called the "transfiguration" of Christ. Jesus took Peter, John, and James—His "inner circle" of disciples, those among the twelve apostles who were the closest to Him—with Him to the top of a mountain to pray.

This, it turned out, would be like no prayer meeting any of these men had seen or would ever see again! Before their very eyes, God spectacularly affirmed His Son's identity:

As he was praying, the appearance of his face changed, and his clothes became as bright as a flash of lightning. Two men, Moses and Elijah, appeared in glorious splendor, talking with Jesus. They spoke about his departure, which he was about to bring to fulfillment at Jerusalem.

Luke 9:29–31

This was a watershed moment, both in Jesus' ministry and in the lives of these three men. And it's also an example of how God will take leaders to mountaintops for the purpose of showing us something special and spectacular about Himself.

The pressure to find an investor to rescue Vanguard was at that time almost unbearable. Cash ran low, and vendors, shareholders, and employees grew increasingly edgy.

I want to close this chapter by telling you about how God did just that for me.

My Own Mountaintop Experience

Priscilla and I have had many "mountaintop" experiences with God. On several occasions, we have traveled to the tops of mountains, where God made His presence in our lives very real to us. However, none of our experiences was more dramatic than the one we enjoyed on Colorado's Pikes Peak just weeks before Vanguard Airlines ceased operation.

As you might imagine, the pressure to find an investor to rescue Vanguard was at that time almost unbearable. Cash ran low, and vendors, shareholders, and employees grew increasingly edgy. More than ever, I needed God's perspective, and He opened a remarkable window for me to get it.

Badly needing a break from all the pressure involved in trying to keep Vanguard afloat, Priscilla and I took a weekend trip to Colorado Springs. On Saturday of that weekend, we decided to travel up Pikes Peak, and we made reservations in the afternoon for a little cog railway that travels from Manitou Springs to the fourteen-thousand-foot summit.

That morning, we drove up to Woodland Park, a small town in the mountains behind Pikes Peak. It wasn't the first time I had been there. One summer when I was a boy, I visited Woodland Park with my parents, sister, and grandparents. I had fond memories of the little town, and I was amazed to find the very house we had stayed in.

As Priscilla and I drove back down the pass from Woodland Park to Colorado Springs, we noticed that the summit of Pikes Peak was enveloped in its usual afternoon cloud cover. Our drive took us past a little gift shop that my mother and grandmother had loved that summer so many years ago. Twenty-five years later, the shop was still there, which amazed me, considering that we live in a time of business failures.

Priscilla loves browsing, so we stopped at the gift shop. I found it to be very much as I had remembered it, except that a large portion of the shop had been converted into a gallery for the artwork of Thomas Kinkade, the world-renowned Christian artist who is known as the "Painter of Light" for his remarkable ability to illuminate various aspects of his works.

Priscilla and I quickly found ourselves in different parts of the shop. I drifted into one of the gallery rooms, where I felt such a presence of God that I began to weep. After a few minutes, I went to find Priscilla, then led her back into the gallery and told her what had happened to me there.

Priscilla had been in the same room just a few minutes before me, admiring a beautiful piece entitled *Perseverance*. It depicted a sailboat struggling through rough water, while in the distant background, the sea was noticeably calmer. The boat's sailor was doing all that he could to move toward the calm water. Kinkade's shading on the picture brought out a halo of light around the boat.

At that very moment, Priscilla and I both knew what God was saying to us through this picture. He wanted us to know that He was present in our lives, urging us to persevere through the struggles at Vanguard. We were reminded that with God at our side, nothing would overcome us. That painting now hangs in our family room as a constant reminder to never give up, even in the hardest times.

To us, God's presence on the peak was tangible.

We drove from the gift shop to Manitou Springs and took the cog train up to the summit of Pikes Peak, all the while feeling that there was something more God wanted to do.

The restaurant and gift shop at the summit were packed with tourists. We halfheartedly browsed the gift shop, then stepped out into the parking lot. We sat down on a large rock near the edge of the lot and began praying together for Vanguard, for our family, and for whatever else God brought to mind.

Suddenly we looked up and saw that the cloud cover above the peak had parted into a perfect circle, forming what looked like a halo over the mountain, several thousand feet above the summit. No one else seemed to notice or care about this scene, but to Priscilla and me, it was one of the clearest channels of communication with God that we could remember.

To us, God's presence on the peak was tangible.

We prayed and told God of our dreams, desires, and needs and praised Him for giving us such a rare opportunity to commune with Him. We thanked Him for what He planned to do with Vanguard and with each of its employees. I trembled as tears ran down my face during those blessed moments.

What were the end results of our mountaintop experience? By now you know that the airline was not saved. But that was not God's purpose for our experience that day. He simply wanted us to know how much He loved us and that He had a plan that extended far beyond saving a company. We realized that His timing and purposes superseded ours and that His plan would ultimately prove to be the better one.

God's presence lingered with Priscilla and me, giving us strength for the company's shutdown and the following weeks of trying to help employees, and ourselves, get our lives back in order.

As leaders, when we are going through the stress of difficult times, we need to seek out the quiet times with God as well as the "mountaintop" times when He brings us close to Himself and teaches us truths about Himself and His love for us. When we do that, we get our perspective aligned with His. When that happens, the blessings are sure to follow.

Principle 4:

PROVIDE "FRONT-LINE" LEADERSHIP

Follow my example, as I follow the example of Christ.

1 Corinthians 11:1

I SPENT NEARLY A DECADE AT my first airline job with American Airlines, one of the largest carriers in the world. I worked with both the parent company and several of its subsidiaries. It was during this time in my career that I witnessed some of the best corporate leadership I have ever seen. . .and some of the worst.

This airline had mastered technological innovation, and I learned much about developing strategic and tactical plans while leveraging technology in amazing ways. Nonetheless, I quickly realized that this airline was renowned for what might fairly be called "steely" treatment of customers. This company didn't always operate by the old business adage "The customer is always right." In fact, there were times when I wondered if our customer service staff realized that ultimately it was the passengers who made their positions with American possible.

In hindsight, I can easily see why this happened. You see, it all started at the top.

AN EXAMPLE OF HOW *NOT* TO MANAGE

> The CEO's personality and management style had percolated throughout the organization.

The CEO of American Airlines at this time had a well-earned reputation as one of the sharpest and most innovative men in the history of the industry, and his approach to both business and people—employees and passengers alike—was mirrored throughout the organization. He was numbers- and technology-driven, which is not necessarily a bad thing for a corporate leader. What was unfortunate, however, was that he also seemed to believe in "management by intimidation." On the few occasions I met him personally, he was cordial. Nonetheless, I had heard the stories of his many tirades in the executive office.

Sadly, this man had personally selected a number of senior executives to mentor, and they, in turn, exhibited many of his same characteristics and behaviors. In effect, the CEO's personality and management style had percolated throughout the organization over the decade-plus he was at the helm. Under his leadership, the executive office, the boardroom, and on-the-line (where the customer meets the employees) frequently became scenes of conflict.

During the latter part of the 1990s, the airline industry prospered, and American Airlines was no exception. But in the early years of the new millennium—a time of great crisis in the airline industry—my old employer was wracked by all kinds of problems with employees and customers. By this time, the CEO I had worked under had retired and been replaced by another man—one of his own choosing. The new CEO was very capable in his own right. However, the problems among the employees and customers persisted. Now, despite the fact that half a decade has passed since the retirement of the dominant CEO, the airline still reflects his personality—both the good and the bad.

I saw during my employment with American Airlines and afterward an example of this one simple truth about business leadership: Organizations are defined by their leaders.

THE DEFINING EFFECT OF LEADERSHIP

Corporate and organizational leaders tend to hire and train people in their own image. If the leadership is "people oriented"—compassionate, polite, attentive, and other things people need to be if they are to enjoy success in business—then that will be reflected in how the lower-level employees deal with the company's or organization's customers.

> A significant test of leadership is how well your employees conduct themselves when new customers disappear, revenue slumps, and creditors breathe down your neck.

The corollary to this is that employees tend to take on the characteristics of their company's leadership. So if the corporate leadership is impersonal and calculating in its dealings with the employees, then customer service will probably not be that company's strong point. On the other hand, if a company's leadership is people oriented, then that company's employees are more likely to be more customer oriented.

For this reason, if a corporate leader wants a company that not only is technically excellent and well schooled in the elements of a particular business or industry but also demonstrates a high level of customer service, then he or she as a leader needs to set the pace.

A significant test of leadership is how well your employees conduct themselves when new customers disappear, revenue slumps, and creditors breathe down your neck looking to be paid. These are the times when you as the leader must tangibly demonstrate how you want your company to behave toward customers and toward one another.

Obviously, the ideal balance within a corporate culture is one in which the company highly values its employees and customers while at the same time producing solid results—in other words, profits. I have also come to believe that this can happen only when corporate leaders take the time to know their employees in an up close and personal way. I believe this means taking time to break down the barriers that often separate corporate leadership and its front-line employees.

BARRIER-BREAKING LEADERSHIP

I have always admired the executives who spend time on the front lines with their employees. One great example of this kind of leadership was a man named Karsten Solheim, the inventor of PING golf clubs and founder of Karsten Manufacturing, an Arizona-based company that produces PING clubs and other golf equipment. Solheim had a management style that was truly ahead of its time.

In the biographical book *Karsten's Way* appears this "nutshell" account of Solheim's management style:

> *He was the owner of Karsten Manufacturing. Everyone who worked there, from the time there were fifteen employees early on to the time the payroll swelled to more than two thousand people, knew that Karsten Solheim was the boss. He may have been one of the most visible bosses in the history of American business. He was in the plant early every day, walking around, checking out how things were going, talking with people, giving instructions, and in general just being as visible and accessible as he could be. Karsten was a master at MBWA—Management By Walking Around.* (Tracy Sumner, *Karsten's Way* [Chicago: Northfield Publishing, 2000], 183.)

No leader is perfect, and that includes Karsten Solheim. But he understood something that we all need to realize, and that's the fact that running a successful business means taking some time on the front lines. The results spoke for themselves. Under his leadership, Karsten Manufacturing was a place where the corporate leaders, management, and employees enjoyed prosperity and also a place where the front-line workers felt valued and appreciated.

This is very much like the kind of leadership I've tried to demonstrate in my career as a CEO. I've found that, while leading in this way may cut into a few golf games or social events, it is well worth the effort. How else can a leader get to know and understand his or her employees on a personal basis? How else can a leader communicate to these people in a tangible way that he or she cares not just about the business but about the people who make that business go? How else can the leader model the type of attitude and behavior he or she wants the company's employees to demonstrate toward each other and toward customers? How else can the leader break down the barriers that so often seem to stand between leadership and the front-line workers?

Over the course of my three-decade career in the transportation industry, I've found that this is the kind of leadership I need to demonstrate on the job.

FRONT-LINE LEADERSHIP IN THE PUBLIC TRANSPORTATION SECTOR

My initial foray into breaking down barriers between management and front-line employees came in the late 1970s, when I was working in the world of public transportation—specifically with urban buses and bus routes. After a short time at this job, I became the manager responsible for the planning and scheduling of a fleet of about a thousand buses plying the streets of Minneapolis–St. Paul, Minnesota.

At the time, this was very difficult work. Personal computers were not in use then; people had to hand-collect data and write it on large ledger sheets. There were no global positioning systems to track the movement of the vehicles; if you wanted to know if a bus was on schedule, you either rode it and compared actual versus scheduled times of arrival at various checkpoints or you jumped in a car and followed the bus as it trundled along its route.

> We had about a dozen people available to monitor more than one hundred bus routs and one thousand buses in a geographic area of about twelve hundred square miles.

My staff and I were charged with trying to optimize ridership, running the buses on time, and providing as much service throughout a large urban area as a perpetually limited public transportation budget would permit. This was immensely labor-intensive work. We had about a dozen people available to monitor more than one hundred bus routes and one thousand buses in a geographic area of about twelve hundred square miles. My small team simply could not cover enough ground.

One day, I had an idea. I was going to start relating in a more personal way with the front-line workers—in this case the fifteen hundred or so men and women who drove the buses. Our metropolitan bus system included four garages where the buses were housed and maintained and where hundreds of drivers began and ended their workdays. I realized that the drivers represented a great source of information we could use to improve the bus system. They certainly had the most detailed knowledge of the routes, where most of their passengers boarded, the driving conditions, and whether they could safely adhere to the schedules produced at headquarters.

A century-long tradition had pitted management (the planners) and union (the drivers) against one another.

I devised a simple system: I and members of my staff would take turns spending one day a month at a bus garage talking to the drivers about how we could improve service. It may not sound all that complicated, but nothing like that had ever been done before. In fact, it ran counter to the culture of public work. A century-long tradition had pitted management (the planners) and union (the drivers) against one other. The two "sides" rarely got together, and when they did, it was to renegotiate contracts or to go over the endless lists of grievances.

Naturally, the drivers were skeptical when management began approaching them and asking questions. As a group, they doubted that anything they told us would make much of a difference. I knew I had barriers to break down, so I made sure that every driver who voiced his or her ideas or concerns received a written reply containing specific reasons why we could or could not make their suggested changes.

As the drivers discovered that we managers were sincere and that we were faithfully showing up at the garage once a day every month to talk to them, we began collecting a lot of valuable data and suggestions. Of course, we also received some dubious information and ideas, mostly from drivers who were less than endeared to us management types. This feedback was fairly easy to discern as being fact or fiction. We used the data and suggestions the drivers provided to help us in our efforts to run the bus service on time and to spot potential trouble before it became serious.

What was most important to me at this time in my career was the fact that our contact with the drivers began breaking down barriers between management and the rank and file. It was in many ways a small effort, but it proved to a group of employees that we as managers had real understanding and compassion for them and for their work.

This experience showed me as a manager the value of taking the time to break down barriers with my front-line employees by getting out there on the front lines. Unfortunately, it was not until nearly two decades later that I could again use this "new" management technique.

FRONT-LINE CONTACT IN THE AIRLINE INDUSTRY

Starting in 1998, I spent three crazy years working as vice

president of planning and revenue management for Grupo TACA, the airline based in Central America. The challenge my family and I faced at that time was that the schools in El Salvador didn't offer everything my children needed. That and the fact that one of my sons had some very special needs at that time meant that my family could not move with me to Central America.

For that reason, I had to commute almost every weekend between El Salvador and my home in Dallas—fifteen hundred miles and seven hours door-to-door each way—so that I could spend time with my family. Fortunately, Grupo TACA had flights between El Salvador and Dallas–Ft. Worth, with an intermediate stop in Guatemala.

As you might expect, my commutes meant spending a lot of time at airports and on airplanes. After a few of those commutes, I decided that I needed to do something to keep my sanity and to make myself useful.

> In the course of each weekly round-trip, I interacted with fifteen to twenty airport personnel, four cockpit crews, and two to four crews of flight attendants. I can hardly count the benefits of this kind of front-line management.

As was typical in many Latin American airlines, communication between corporate officers and rank-and-file employees at Grupo TACA was minimal. So I decided to change that, at least as much as one VP could. In doing so, I would have some fun, make some new friends, learn from our employees, and help out in any way I could.

My routine eventually included showing up a few hours early for my flight from El Salvador to Guatemala. Instead of using that time to relax or catch up on my reading, I went to the gate area where our flights arrived and departed and helped out with gate-area duties, such as answering customer questions, guiding passengers to their flights, and collecting tickets at the jet bridge.

From there, I got on my flight and took the forty-minute hop to the airport in Guatemala, where I would visit the boarding lounge and help our Guatemalan staff with many of the same duties I had helped out with in El Salvador. I then got back on the plane for my flight to Dallas–Ft. Worth. On that flight, I would ride in the cockpit and talk with the pilots and help flight attendants with simple galley chores and listen to their needs and concerns. I would also talk with customers, do some of my own work, and read. On the flight back to El Salvador, I would do the same things, only in reverse order.

In the course of each weekly round-trip, I interacted with fifteen to twenty airport personnel, four cockpit crews, two to four crews of flight attendants (there was usually a crew change in Guatemala), and any number of passengers.

I can hardly count the benefits of this kind of front-line management. I recognized customer-handling procedures that needed correcting, and I saw routes that included too little or too much flying time. I heard what customers liked and disliked about our airline, and I taught our staff how to solve certain types of customer service problems on the spot.

More important, I was able to show our airline workers that senior management—at least *this* senior manager—cared. Few of my fellow corporate officers spent this kind of time in the trenches.

In time, I came to personally know a couple hundred employees—many of them Guatemalan—who had little or no contact with headquarters. This gave me the opportunity to find out what was going on in the lives of the front-line people, the ones who, when everything was said and done, made the airline go. I learned about who was sick, whose parent had died, who was getting married, who had had a baby, and who was discouraged. In the process, I found out who our best employees were, but more important to me, I showed them that I really cared about them.

When it comes to running what was then about a $600-million-a-year airline, this might not seem like such a big deal. But it gave me as a leader a chance to demonstrate compassion and to learn and teach. That meant a lot to me, and it meant a lot to the people with whom I came into contact during my journeys to and from El Salvador.

Our VP of human resources and legal counsel worked on a ramp, loading and unloading bags.

ON THE FRONT LINE AT VANGUARD

After seeing and living with the benefits of spending quality time with employees in their day-to-day work environment at Grupo TACA, I was determined to put into place a comprehensive plan of this kind when I took over at Vanguard Airlines. In fact, my time with the Kansas City–based airline afforded me my greatest opportunity to date to put my theories to the test. This time, however, I was determined to make this management style a part of the larger culture at Vanguard.

In one of my early staff meetings at Vanguard, I asked the corporate officers to each find something they could do to help our front-line employees at some time during the week. I'm happy to report that they went above and beyond the call of duty in doing so. For example, our vice president of planning and revenue management took calls at the reservations center, and our VP of human resources and legal counsel worked on a ramp, loading and unloading bags. Several other vice presidents pitched in with airport check-in at our Kansas City hub. Our vice president of operations, who had logged thousands of hours as pilot-in-command of large transports, periodically flew scheduled flights.

The presence of these corporate officers on the front lines meant a lot to the employees and to the passengers. It meant a lot to me, too, especially since everyone who participated in these activities kept their work priorities straight. Their first priority was to perform their "normal" duties and to perform them well and completely. That they did!

Vanguard's corporate offices were less than a half mile from our gates at the Kansas City airport, so I was able to drive over to the terminal after hours and help out at night, early in the morning, or on weekends. I started out by just standing behind our passenger check-in counter, watching the process, and helping our agents move bags onto the conveyor belt that took them down to the bag room. I have always been good at using technology, so I also learned how to check in passengers on our airport computer system. In time, I learned to perform many of the duties of a passenger service agent.

On heavy travel days—in the summer and around major holidays like Thanksgiving and Christmas—most of the corporate officers, as well as many headquarters staff, turned out to help check in passengers and their bags, answer questions, and board and unload flights.

All of this created a very strong atmosphere of "family" at Vanguard. It also gave me the opportunity to learn a great deal about our people, our customers, and the needs and desires of both. And it gave me the opportunity to talk with at least a few employees several times a week. That allowed me to quell the many rumors about Vanguard and to provide factual information much more effectively than I could have by just issuing written bulletins or sending e-mails.

Most important, however, I also was able to model the type of customer service we needed to provide, especially when we entered into a "sink or swim" mode after September 11.

GOING THE EXTRA MILE IN TOUGH TIMES

Like most airlines, Vanguard often had to deal with weather-related issues. When winter weather shut down one of the airports we served, we had passengers who needed our assistance finding overnight lodging wherever they were stuck. In such cases, the customer must pay for his or her room for the night. However, if the fault for the delays lay with the airline—mechanical problems, for example—the airline picked up the tab for the hotel.

> One of our passenger service agents took me aside and informed me that there was a woman sitting off to the side crying.

Early on in my time with Vanguard, a heavy snowfall in Buffalo, New York, caused the cancellation of one of our flights. That night, I was working in the airport in Kansas City, and one of our passenger service agents took me aside and informed me that there was a woman sitting off to the side crying. The agent had asked the woman what was wrong, and she said she had spent all her money on a ticket to fly from a city in the west via Kansas City to Buffalo and had nothing left for a hotel room. She lived in another city and knew no one in Kansas City, so she faced the prospect of spending twenty-four hours in the airport with no place to sleep.

Our agent knew it was not official company policy to provide stranded passengers lodging when the cancellation or delay was weather related. But feeling the kind of compassion

I would want any of our employees to feel for someone in such a jam, the agent asked me if we could make an exception for this woman and put her up in a local motel. I readily agreed that we should do just that. The woman, as you might imagine, was most thankful.

That same evening, another woman bound for Buffalo was stuck at the airport. Her family had driven her to the Kansas City airport from a small town about twenty-five miles to the north, then left her there. For some reason, she could not reach anyone in the family, had no money other than what was available for the ticket, and faced a night in the airport. Without me saying anything, another of our customer service agents volunteered to drive her the twenty-five miles back home as soon as her shift ended. I felt pride and genuine joy at seeing that agent's act of kindness toward that woman, and I realized that compassion for others truly can be contagious.

> Every business has its down cycles, and corporate leadership needs to display grace, compassion, and more business acumen during difficult times.

Operating a business with compassion and developing good customer service sometimes involves making exceptions, going out of your way, or going the extra mile. It was gratifying to me to be able to do good for others who were in a jam, even when we were not legally or contractually obligated to do so.

To this day, I believe that the people at Vanguard did those things out of a sense of compassion built through the extra effort made by the company's management team.

That was the way I wanted to run our business, and I believe that if you do the same, you'll see the same kinds of compassionate customer service on the part of your business's employees.

But remember, as you spend time with your employees in their work environment in good times, you should redouble your efforts during the bad times. When I was with Vanguard, it was relatively easy and fun for me to work behind the ticket counter when the airline carried lots of people and the planes ran on schedule. Every business has its down cycles, and corporate leadership needs to display grace, compassion, and more business acumen during difficult times.

Believe me, your employee will love you and be all the more loyal to you if you take time on the front lines during the tough times.

Let's take a look at some practical ways you can demonstrate front-line leadership.

SOME KEYS FOR FRONT-LINE LEADERSHIP

Front-line leadership requires special effort. It requires you to do things that some managers and leaders might find unorthodox or downright strange. But I have found front-line leadership to be both effective and a personal blessing—to me and to those who have worked under me. So here are some keys to front-line leadership:

1. *Front-line leadership means going out of your way.* If you want to lead on the front lines of your company or corporation, it will mean getting away from the office—away from the meetings, away from the conferences, away from the phone calls and e-mails—and getting out there. That may not be easy for you to do; in fact, it might be downright inconvenient. But it will be worth the effort, particularly when your company is going through difficult times.

2. *Front-line leadership involves becoming personally involved with those you are leading.* It's part of human nature to want to work harder and better for someone when you know that they actually care about you as a person. For that reason, I believe good front-line leadership means doing all you can to become personally involved, as much as it is possible and appropriate, in the lives of the people who work under you. That means taking a personal interest in their successes and failures, their joys and heartaches, and their worries and concerns.

You can't have a "do as I say, not as I do" attitude when it comes to front-line leadership.

One of the reasons I chose to get out there on the front lines was that I wanted to demonstrate that I cared personally about the people who worked for me and that I appreciated the things they did to make the organization I was working for at the time a success. One of the benefits of doing that, I found out, was that the people who worked under me found out that I was "for real" and responded to me with greater loyalty.

3. *Front-line leadership means encouraging other leaders to join you.* This means leading by example. You can't have a "do as I say, not as I do" attitude when it comes to front-line leadership. On the contrary, you must show yourself willing to do what you are asking others to do. I personally believe that encouraging others to join you in front-line leadership means first going out ahead of them and doing it, then encouraging them to join you. So do all you can to encourage those officers and others who work under you to go out to the front lines, but make sure they know that it's a "team effort," one that you are willing to personally join.

4. *Front-line leadership means setting an example by treating customers and clients the way you want those who work under you to treat them.* Can you imagine what would happen if the manager or officer of a company demonstrated an attitude of indifference or even disdain toward those the company was there to serve? I can tell you from experience that an attitude like that on the part of the leadership trickles down to those who work on the front lines.

On the other hand, when a leader demonstrates an attitude of cheerful service, of patience, of compassion, and of concern that customers or clients are happy with the service they receive, those on the front lines will almost always have the same attitude.

Finally, front-line leadership means taking the time and effort to communicate effectively and honestly with those you are leading. Let's examine what it takes to communicate that way with those who are important to your success.

PRINCIPLE 5:

COMMUNICATE— OFTEN AND HONESTLY

A truthful witness gives honest testimony,
but a false witness tells lies.

PROVERBS 12:17

As the Revolutionary War

drew to a close, General George Washington penned a letter to the governors of the thirteen newly freed states titled "Circular Letter Addressed to the Governors of all the States on the Disbanding of the Army." The letter is also known as Washington's "Earnest Prayer."

This was on the eve of one of the greatest political experiments in history, the founding of a truly democratic nation. In the letter, Washington implored the leaders of our country to conduct themselves in a manner honoring of God and to do it in a cooperative and understanding way:

> *I now make it my earnest prayer that God would have you, and the State over which you preside, in his holy protection; that he would incline the hearts of the citizens to cultivate a spirit of subordination and obedience to government, to entertain a brotherly affection and*

love for one another, for their fellow-citizens of the United States at large, and particularly for brethren who have served in the field; and finally that he would most graciously be pleased to dispose us all to do justice, to love mercy, and to demean ourselves with that charity, humility, and pacific temper of mind, which were the characteristics of the Divine Author of our blessed religion, and without an humble imitation of whose example in these things, we can never hope to be a happy nation.

Washington's words were both inspirational and prophetic. His advice was followed in fits and starts, but in general it was followed. Because of that, the greatest nation in history emerged over the coming century.

But the general's words were not only inspirational; they were also an example of a leader taking the time to communicate his vision, in this case a vision of the founding and growth of a great nation.

I believe it is important that leaders follow this example, and I believe it is especially important to follow it when times are tough.

WHEN COMMUNICATION GOES AWRY

I recently had the opportunity to spend a number of months working with a Latin American airline, although not the same one I worked for in El Salvador. Part of my job was to observe the operations and management as a representative of the airline's primary creditor.

> The managers didn't seem to want to, or even know how to, communicate with the lower-level employees.

As I observed the airline's operations, I found out that due to a wide variety of circumstances, the airline faced considerable financial distress. Although the problems were fairly serious, I believed that they were solvable—*if* everyone pulled together toward that goal.

I got to know many people throughout the organization—from the CEO to the senior management to the pilots, flight attendants, analysts, and airport customer service staff. I observed that the airline's employees had been reasonably well trained. In general, they did good work. However, I also observed that the airline's management team was not one of the more "enlightened" I had ever seen.

What was this management team's problem? Simply put, the managers didn't seem to want to, or even know how to, communicate with the lower-level employees. They communicated with employees on very rare occasions and usually only when some dire crisis precipitated that communication. The employees hungered for information on the state of their airline, but management mostly said nothing, leaving the employees in the dark. Consequently, rumors ran rampant, and morale sank to the point where the employees seemed to be losing interest in their work.

I believed then, and still believe now, that when a business or company is going through difficult times, it is vital for management to go out of its way to communicate with its employees. For that reason, I strongly urged this airline's management to do just that. Unfortunately, I was the proverbial "voice crying in the wilderness." Try as I might, I couldn't seem to persuade that airline's managers to get out there with the troops and communicate regularly and truthfully.

I didn't believe for a minute that the lack of internal communication within this struggling airline was a cultural difference. I remembered well that the airline I worked for in El Salvador did an ever-improving job of internal communications during my tenure. No, this was a simple and tragic case of managers who didn't know how to—or weren't willing to—communicate at a time when the employees needed more than anything to hear from their bosses.

The consequences of this lack of communication were what I might have expected. The airline's performance deteriorated measurably, and it quickly slipped into a very precarious position. As the problems deepened, the airline's on-time arrival rate declined by about 25 percent to completely unacceptable levels. Customer complaints became more and more common as the airport passenger service agents began displaying indifference and even outright rudeness to those who ultimately paid the bills: the passengers themselves. Sadly, cessation of operations followed not too long afterward.

It was a textbook case of how *not* to run an airline—or any business, for that matter.

> Employees are often starved for news about the general state of the business that employs them.

THE BENEFITS OF GOOD COMMUNICATION

As someone who has worked a great number of years in senior management, I have observed that poor communication can be part of a vicious cycle that can quickly sink an already struggling business.

I have also learned that it is possible to alleviate employee stress and sustain a business through hard times. But that can happen only when that business's leadership is willing to communicate effectively with its staff, shareholders, vendors, and everyone else who has a stake in the company's operations.

Employees are often starved for news about the general state of the business that employs them. This is particularly true when the business is going through a downtime. When management fails to communicate with its employees at times like these, it creates an atmosphere of uncertainty, and that's an atmosphere in which stress, anxiety, high turnover, and poor-quality service thrive. That's because it is difficult, if not impossible, for many employees to do their jobs and do them well when they don't know what's really going on with the company.

For these reasons, I would recommend to any business leader that he or she make good communication a part of his or her personal management style. But how does a manager do this effectively?

THE LOOK OF GOOD COMMUNICATION

As CEO of Vanguard Airlines, I was committed to making communication with my employees, as well as fellow managers and others involved with the company, a priority. I did that using traditional methods: memos, e-mails, phone calls, and regular personal appearances. And I also did that by using some basic guidelines I've developed over the course of my career in management.

Here are those guidelines:

Guideline 1: Communicate truthfully, even when it's painful to do so. There's something about human nature that makes most of us reluctant or completely unwilling to give people disturbing news. Indeed, it's never easy to have to tell people that your company or organization is struggling. But I've found that it's better to let people know up front what kind of struggles you are really facing than to put a "happy face" on things.

We all agreed that we would give our employees, our shareholders, and media the truth—no matter how good or bad it was.

This may sound like a no-brainer, but it's amazing how

many executives, as well as other business leaders, alter or omit facts in an attempt to pacify or comfort anxious or stressed-out people—their employees as well as others associated with their companies—rather than giving them the plain truth. In the end, however, this kind of deception only brings the business leader trouble, as it breeds a climate of mistrust on the part of those around the leader.

At Vanguard, I and my team of corporate officers were committed to leading with integrity, so we all agreed that we would give our employees, our shareholders, and media the truth—no matter how good or bad it was—and give it on a timely basis.

There were several reasons for this, the first and foremost of them being that it was the right thing to do. As a business leader who wants more than anything to please God in everything I do, I can't allow my fear of giving people bad news to keep me from being honest about the state of our company.

Today's legal environment requires publicly traded companies to supply written and timely disclosures of all significant events and conditions that could affect the financial and operational performance of those companies. Fulfillment of these regulations can be a real burden, but in reality, it forces companies to communicate truthfully. But as godly businesses leaders, we shouldn't need corporate laws or regulations to motivate us to communicate honestly. For us, that motivation comes out of a heart that loves God and that is compassionately concerned with the well-being of our employees, stockholders, vendors, and customers.

When I think of this kind of communication, I'm reminded of some of the words of Winston Churchill, who when he took over as prime minister of Great Britain had as much reason as anyone to sugarcoat the truth. Instead, however, Churchill was honest—brutally honest—when he told the people, "I have nothing to offer but blood, toil, tears, and sweat." Never were truer words spoken. Over the next few years, the height of World War II, the British people would be faced with a fight for their very survival as a nation, and they needed to know the truth about their situation.

> Jesus was honest about the situation the disciples would face, and He wanted them to know up front that they would face difficulties as they sought to serve Him.

I am also motivated toward being truthful about the situations of the companies I work for by the honest and difficult words of Jesus as He sent His disciples out to serve on His behalf:

"I am sending you out like sheep among wolves. Therefore be as shrewd as snakes and as innocent as doves.

But be on guard against men; they will hand you over to the local councils and flog you in their synagogues. On my account you will be brought before

governors and kings as witnesses to them and to the
Gentiles."

MATTHEW 10:16–18

Jesus was honest about the situation the disciples would face, and He wanted them to know up front that they would face difficulties as they sought to serve Him. As business leaders who want to please Him, we should do no less when it comes to our own "disciples."

Guideline 2: Don't give away confidences. While we as business leaders should strive to be open and honest about the state of our companies or corporations, we should know that there are certain situations in which we need to keep confidences with others.

Here is an example of what I'm talking about:

After September 11, Vanguard Airline's officers and employees knew the airline industry was in trouble, and they knew that our airline was no exception. They also knew that in order for Vanguard to survive, it needed an infusion of capital from the outside. Two broad sources of capital were available at that time: private investment from a venture capitalist or something similar, or a government-sponsored loan guarantee.

As we in senior management sought this new infusion of capital, we issued frequent updates to our employees, stockholders, and vendors alike. But because our potential private investors wanted anonymity during this process, we were limited in what we could tell people about our pursuit of capital from these sources. We couldn't tell people who we were talking to about private funding or the details of those talks. What we could tell them about, however, was the progress we were making, or not making, toward acquiring the new capital we so desperately needed. That we did—but very carefully.

The federal government loan guarantee option that we pursued, on the other hand, was a very public process. The applications for the loan guarantee program were being examined and approved by a tripartite group of three federal agencies—the Departments of Transportation and Treasury plus the Federal Reserve Board. Since these deliberations were semipublic, we on Vanguard's corporate leadership team felt much freer to communicate the progress—or lack thereof—we were making in securing a guaranteed loan. At a couple points during the loan guarantee application process, we even urged our employees to contact their elected officials and ask them to put pressure on the government departments on our behalf.

Imagine what it would be like to work for a company whose leaders communicated with you and your coworkers three or four times one month, not at all the next month, twice the month after that, then not at all the month following.

When it comes to what you can and cannot tell your employees, stockholders, and vendors concerning the inner workings and financial state of your company, be honest, but use your judgment and common sense. If you aren't sure whether or not you should disclose something, seek legal counsel.

Guideline 3: Communicate regularly. I believe that if there is one thing worse than no communication at all, it's hit-or-miss communication. Let me illustrate what I mean:

Imagine what it would be like to work for a company whose leaders communicated with you and your coworkers three or four times one month, not at all the next month, twice the month after that, then not at all the month following. How do you think that would make you feel? Nervous? Anxious? Insecure? All of the above? Believe me, if you had any of these emotional responses, you wouldn't be alone. I'd daresay that most, if not all, of your coworkers would feel exactly the same way.

That is exactly what I observed working with the Latin American airline I mentioned earlier in this chapter. The erratic communication on the part of that airline's management team caused a lot of fear and uncertainty among the front-line workers. The longer the managers went between times of communication, the more the rumors began to surface, and that resulted in poor morale and, consequently, poor customer service.

During difficult times especially, it is absolutely crucial that the leaders of a particular business provide their employees updates and that they do it regularly. Unfortunately, however, there are many corporate leaders who communicate only when there is something positive or good to tell their employees and others connected to the company. I've seen up close and personally that this is death to any business.

So make sure that you as a business leader communicate *regularly*. Whether you provide updates weekly (I've found that to be the optimum), twice monthly, or monthly, make sure that you give those updates when the people in your company have come to expect them.

Guideline 4: As much as you can, communicate on a personal level. There is no better communication than the personal kind. That includes in your personal relationships and in your business relationships as well. In a large organization, personalized communication is no easy task, but opportunities to communicate personally will present themselves—if the business leader watches for them.

> As a business leader, communicating on a personal level with the people in your company will help build a corporate environment of openness and honesty.

My secretary at Vanguard Airlines, along with other staff, helped me in this area by keeping me informed about the significant personal events in the lives of employees—events such as births, deaths of loved ones, medical situations, weddings, family crises, and other big events. My wife also assisted me greatly in this regard. She periodically passed through the offices just to say "hello" to the staff there. When she did that, she drew much out of people—their joys and sorrows, their hurts and hopes, their defeats and victories—to pray about. She constantly encouraged people, and she also let me know (of course, keeping the confidences she was asked to keep) when one of our employees was going through something important or difficult. This sensitivity provided the opportunity for me to personally visit with that person in need and to offer him or her my support in prayer. It also gave me the opportunity to communicate face-to-face with employees concerning the state of the airline. More important, it allowed me the chance to let these people know that, even though I was the boss and was concerned with the day-to-day operations of the airline, I cared personally for them.

As a business leader, communicating on a personal level with the people in your company will help build a corporate environment of openness and honesty. As much as you can, take the time to communicate with your people this way, and encourage your fellow officers or managers to do the same. You and your employees will reap great rewards when you do so.

Guideline 5: Bring God into the communication picture. As you as a godly business leader take the steps to make good, honest communication a part of the climate in which your business operates, it's important to bring God and His ways into your communication.

I believe you can do that by taking two steps: First,

make sure your employees and others know that you are praying for them and that you care about them. Second, ask them to pray about the issues your company faces. More often than not, you'll find that they'll appreciate your prayers and concerns and that they'll be willing to pray for your business. After all, what happens to and in your business affects them, too!

During most of my communications with employees at Vanguard, I urged them to pray for the airline. While I am sure that some "skeptics" in the company didn't necessarily appreciate this part of my communication with them, I also know that during the course of our ten-month effort to survive, I did not receive one complaint concerning my requests for prayer. On the contrary, I received many compliments and much encouragement from people for doing so. I also know that as I shared with the employees our company's concerns and at the same time asked them to pray over our needs, I encouraged them to put their focus on God. That, after all, is why He put us here in the first place.

LOVING YOUR NEIGHBOR. . .BY COMMUNICATING

Leaders in difficult situations certainly need strength. I believe that strength comes from the Lord when He is pleased with what we do. And what does He want us first and foremost to do? Love Him with our hearts and love our neighbors (employees) as we love ourselves (Matthew 19:19).

We can do that by regularly communicating with them in an honest, personal, and godly way.

Communicating well is good for business and good for each of us as individuals. But more than that, it's a kind and compassionate thing to do—the *right* thing to do!

PRINCIPLE 6:

PERSEVERE
THROUGH EVERYTHING!

You need to persevere so that
when you have done the will of God,
you will receive what he has promised.

HEBREWS 10:36

MOST OF US KNOW WINSTON

Churchill as the wise and articulate prime minister who led Great Britain through the darkest days of World War II. But what most people don't know is that before Churchill earned global acclaim and a place in the history books for a job well done, his political life was marked by trial, testing, and failure.

During World War I, Churchill served as first lord of admiralty for Great Britain, a position that put him in charge of the world's most powerful navy. It was during this time that Churchill modernized the Royal Navy and set up the Royal Naval Air Service, giving Great Britain the ability to utilize air power.

But it was during this time that Britain suffered through two great military disasters. The first took place when a British fleet engaged a German battle group off the coast of Chile near a place known as Coronel. The British were resoundingly defeated.

The second military debacle took place in Turkey, where the British attempted to unseat the German-Turkish alliance from dominance over the critical Bosphorus region, which gave that alliance control over the sea-lanes between much of Europe and Asia. Churchill endorsed the invasion of the Gallipoli Peninsula, near modern-day Istanbul, by British, Australian, and New Zealand forces. But this incursion was an unprecedented disaster. The Turkish army decimated the Allied troops in a brutal campaign that saw tens of thousands die in a series of ill-conceived and poorly executed engagements. After a few months of the carnage, the Allied troops were withdrawn.

As a result of these failures, public sentiment against Churchill and his advisors reached an all-time high. The future leader of the British Empire was forced to resign his position as lord of the admiralty in disgrace and humiliation.

Yet Churchill did not give up. He persevered in his political career and regained the esteem of the British people. Later, he was named prime minister, giving him the opportunity to lead the British to victory over their Nazi invaders in World War II.

> I've known leaders to absolutely quit when they faced some kind of adversity.

Churchill's political career is an illustration of something we as Christian leaders need to understand, and it's this: Sometimes trials, testings, and failures are preludes to great blessings from the hand of God.

CALLED TO A HIGHER STANDARD

When a leader faces adversity, be it in the form of a business downturn or in the form of an absolute business failure, it's difficult. But when that leader allows himself or herself to give up after a setback, it's tragic.

I've known leaders to absolutely quit when they faced some kind of adversity. Some of them have fallen into debilitating depression, while others have fallen into alcohol or drug abuse, adultery, or illegal or immoral business practices—all in an attempt to dull the pain of their failure or to regain what they have lost.

But those of us leaders who have put our faith in Christ are called to a higher standard of living. We are called to a life that pleases God and opens the way for blessings from Him. And we are to do that in the good times and the bad alike.

But how do we keep ourselves focused on pleasing God when our minds are spinning trying to figure out how to get through our difficult times? I believe that is a matter of knowing first that our trials and failures can in themselves be a blessing simply because they mold our character and faith and make us suitable for God's greater purposes. But we need to take that thinking a step further and realize that the trials and failures we endure—in our personal and spiritual lives as well as our business lives—could well be the path God has chosen to bring us to greater blessings.

I believe now more than ever that God is calling leaders to be people of patience and perseverance. And I also believe

It would require the leadership of a man who could face adversity but keep his eyes on the ultimate prize.

that as we follow that call and allow God to make patience and perseverance part of our character—even in the face of trials and failures—we open ourselves to greater things from Him.

I believe that this principle is demonstrated in scripture, where we can read of the man I see as one of the greatest "CEOs" of all time: Moses.

PERSEVERANCE IN THE WILDERNESS

God had an incredible plan: molding a couple million Jews into a great nation. This would be the fulfillment of a promise He had made to Abraham hundreds of years before, but it would require the leadership of a man who could face adversity but keep his eyes on the ultimate prize.

That man was Moses.

It was a daunting task, to be sure. It would require Moses to demonstrate incredible—almost superhuman—patience and perseverance. He would face many tests and trials on the way, but he knew that there was a huge blessing ahead—if he persevered.

Moses' first step was to set God's people free from the bondage of slavery in Egypt, which was led by a very stubborn Pharaoh, who wasn't going to give up this source of free labor without a fight. Time after time, Moses approached

Pharaoh with this simple message: "Let my people go!" Time after time, however, Pharaoh refused.

But God was on Moses' side. It was only a matter of time—not to mention a matter of plagues of frogs, bugs, blood, hail, and other unpleasant things—before Pharaoh gave in and set the Israelites free.

Though he had liberated his people from bondage, Moses still had many adversities and setbacks ahead of him. He had to lead the people in an unknown wilderness, battle hostile peoples, and deal with the Israelites' rebellion and unbelief. What's more, he'd have to do it for forty years while he and his people wandered in the desert.

As I've read these accounts in the book of Exodus, I've come to the conclusion that Moses was one of the most patient men who ever lived. And I've also come to the conclusion that he passed the virtue of patience on to his successor, Joshua.

Joshua also needed patience and perseverance beyond measure. He had to lead the people into Canaan, where they fought battles against armies that had them badly outnumbered and "outgunned." But Joshua wasn't going to settle for anything less than God's best for him and his people. So he persevered.

What was the end result of all this patience and perseverance? Because Moses and Joshua endured these testings and trials, they were able to lead a nation of people—people who were destined to shake and shape the world for thousands of years to come—into a land of blessing and promise.

Moses and Joshua are well worthy of our admiration for their patience and perseverance in the face of testing and trials. But there is another figure—one of my favorites in history—who demonstrated the same kind of patience and perseverance on the way to accomplishing great things for God.

> Wilberforce resolved that with God's help, he would do everything he could to eliminate slavery from the empire.

THE PERSEVERANCE OF WILLIAM WILBERFORCE

William Wilberforce was an aspiring politician who eventually was elected to a seat in the British Parliament in the late 1700s. From that position, he helped lead the initiative to abolish the slave trade in the British Empire.

Wilberforce had accepted Jesus as his Lord and Savior some years prior to his election, and he was deeply convicted of the abhorrence of the practice of slavery—especially after meeting men like John Newton, the slave-trader-turned-pastor-and-hymn-writer, who talked to Wilberforce about the evils of the trade.

Wilberforce was aware of the commercial impact of slavery in Britain. He knew that many merchants prospered greatly from trafficking in precious souls. But Wilberforce resolved that with God's help, he would do everything he could to eliminate slavery from the empire.

This would be easier said than done. Wilberforce fought a twenty-year battle in Parliament, submitting draft after draft of legislation to repeal the slave trade, only to see every attempt defeated. His fellow parliamentarians resoundingly criticized and ostracized Wilberforce, and the press of the day mocked him to no end.

But Wilberforce didn't give up. He brought other men to his side. These men formed a support group focused on prayer, Bible study, and mutual encouragement. This group became known as the Clapham Sect, so named after the place where they met. The members of this group included other members of Parliament who shared Wilberforce's faith in God. Slowly but surely, the character of Parliament began to change as more men of God filled its ranks.

Nonetheless, Wilberforce didn't secure victory in his battle to abolish slavery—at least not right away. That battle continued in Parliament and throughout British society into the early 1800s.

Finally, the breakthrough came. One night, Wilberforce and his colleagues made one more plea before Parliament to abolish the slave trade in the British Empire. This time, instead of the usual derision from his fellow parliamentarians, man after man arose to speak in support of the abolitionist cause and to praise

> What blessings followed? The redemption of millions from the bonds of slavery.

Wilberforce for his faithfulness and perseverance in the pursuit of righteousness and justice. When the vote was taken, the motion to abolish slavery in the British Empire passed by an enormous margin.

All of Parliament arose to give Wilberforce a tumultuous ovation. The overwhelmed Wilberforce was so exhausted from the years of struggle that he could only sit, with tears streaming down his face, as his colleagues paid tribute to him for his vision and perseverance.

What blessings followed? The redemption of millions from the bonds of slavery. But that wasn't all. In what many believe was a response to Wilberforce's faithfulness and perseverance, God unleashed a revival throughout Great Britain that sparked one of the greatest missionary movements—one that transformed countless millions of lives—in all of history.

William Wilberforce was yet another example of the blessings that come when a leader refuses to give up in his pursuit of righteousness and justice. Instead, he perseveres in the pursuit of what is right.

Not many of us are called to endeavors that require the kind of patience and perseverance that Moses, Joshua, or William Wilberforce needed. But all of us will face situations in which we will need to persevere.

As you have seen throughout this book, I've needed to persevere through some setbacks and failures in my professional life. In my family life, I've had to do the same thing. And just as God blessed me as I persevered at work, He blessed my family as we held fast with our son Patrick.

FACING A FAMILY TRIAL

When I was offered the job with the airline in El Salvador, my wife and I agreed that I should accept the position with the understanding that she and Daniel, our youngest son who was a high school sophomore at the time, would move down and live with me. Our oldest son, David, was already away at college, and our middle son, Patrick, was preparing to leave for his freshman year at a Christian college in a city about 150 miles from home.

> During his first semester at college, Priscilla and I came across the hard evidence we needed to prove that our son was using drugs.

There was, however, an obstacle to that plan.

During Patrick's high school years, his behavior had gone steadily downhill, resulting in frequent arguments and tension at home. Priscilla and I began to suspect that drugs or alcohol were affecting his behavior, but we never found conclusive proof.

Patrick kept his grades up just enough to get into a small college and maintained his abilities as a basketball player just enough to secure a spot on the school's junior varsity team. But during his first semester at college, Priscilla and I came across the hard evidence we needed to prove that our son was using drugs. Everything came to a head during the Christmas holiday after Patrick's first semester. We invited a man who ran a Christian drug rehabilitation program to join our family in an intervention. After an agonizing and tense discussion, Patrick agreed to join the program to get help. He pulled out of school and moved to the rehab center, about seventy-five miles outside Dallas.

But the trials continued to mount for our family. Patrick's situation meant that my wife and youngest son couldn't join me in El Salvador. This was doubly confirmed when we discovered that the high school in El Salvador wasn't suitable for Daniel. It was a good school academically, but it lacked the music and athletic programs that Daniel had enjoyed in Dallas.

After much agonizing and prayer, we decided that Priscilla and Daniel would continue living in Dallas and that I would take the seven-hour commute from El Salvador to be with my family on weekends and to take the drive to the rehab center to see Patrick.

Of course, he took the only seat available—the one next to me.

Still, the trials did not abate. After some months, we discovered that the rehab program wasn't helping Patrick the way we had hoped and prayed it would. Our son and our family needed a breakthrough.

After we visited Patrick one weekend, Priscilla and I—both at our wits' end by this time—drove back to Dallas. As we made our way down the highway, Priscilla and I began praying with great fervency. I do not remember all our words, but I remember that Pris started shouting out loud to God to "do something." I joined her in that same cry.

We had no idea what kind of blessing God was about to unleash.

THE BEGINNING OF A BLESSING

The next morning, I made my usual pilgrimage back to El Salvador. I often flew on Continental Airlines from Dallas to Houston, then connected to El Salvador. My flight to Houston went smoothly, and I was soon seated on a very full flight for El Salvador. The seat next to me was open (it was the only empty seat on the flight), and as the door was about to close, I thought I might get a little elbow room. I settled in and opened an interesting book. Suddenly, a young man was allowed to board. Of course, he took the only seat available— the one next to me.

Almost immediately, I felt the presence of the Lord all around me. There was something very different about the young man sitting next to me. What happened in the next twenty minutes seemed almost surreal, but I soon knew that it was completely God-ordained.

There were rarely "gringos" on this flight, so I assumed that the young man next to me was Salvadoran. However, he spoke to me in flawless English, apologizing for having to take the only open seat on the flight. Then we began a conversation that would be the beginning of God's blessing on my family.

"I see you are reading a Christian book," the young man noticed. "Are you a believer?"

"Yes, I am," I answered. "Are you?"

"Yes," he replied, then identified himself as "Patrick." (In order to protect his identity, I will call him "Patrick Q.")

Patrick Q. told me that he had been working in San Salvador as a youth pastor and that his parents were missionaries there. He had flown to Dallas looking into the possibility of getting more training at a Bible school there. He also told me that he worked part-time as a customer service agent for Continental Airlines.

"That's great!" I said. "I know the school you want to attend, and it's a good one."

I then told Patrick Q. that I had a son named Patrick and that he was about his age. I also told him about what my son was going through at that time.

It didn't make sense at the time, but the conviction that I should offer to help him weighed so heavily on me that I could not contain it.

"He is in a drug rehab center and is not in very good shape," I said. "My wife and I are trusting God to intervene and restore him. I commute back and forth between El Salvador and Dallas every weekend to be with my family and to visit Patrick."

This trip was already starting to look up. My seatmate was a Christian and a youth pastor, and he wanted to go to a Bible college in Dallas that Priscilla and I knew well. I thought that we could perhaps share some fellowship and prayer on the flight.

Then God struck in a way I could hardly believe. Tears came to my eyes as He impressed upon me that I should offer to help this near-stranger through Bible college. But how could that be? I had only known him for about five minutes. I was already supporting one son in college and Patrick at the rehab center. It didn't make sense at the time, but the conviction that I should offer to help him weighed so heavily on me that I could not contain it.

With tears now streaming down my face, I turned to Patrick Q. and said, "I will help put you through Bible college as best I am able."

He was thunderstruck at what I said, and tears came to his eyes, too.

"Do you really mean it?" he asked.

"Yes, I really mean it," I assured him.

The people around Patrick Q. and me probably thought we were nuts. Here we were, two grown men who hardly knew each other, and we were both crying like babies.

Then, as if I wasn't overwhelmed enough, Patrick Q. made my family an offer I knew was directly from God.

"Scott," he said, "when I get to Dallas, I will take your Patrick under my wing and minister to him."

Patrick Q. went on to tell me that he had become addicted to drugs when he was part of the surfing scene in Southern California. Then, several years before our meeting on the flight, God got hold of him, took away his addiction, and told him that he was going to be an evangelist and pastor. Since then, he had been working with drug-addicted kids and gang members through his church in El Salvador.

He took the time to minister to our son and became instrumental in helping him turn his life in the right direction.

At that moment, there was no doubt in my mind that God had responded to Priscilla's and my cry of desperation on behalf of our son. This young man was seated at the last minute in the only empty seat on my flight— *right next to me*—and his name was Patrick, and he had been redeemed from drug addiction and was now serving the Lord. Patrick Q. was, in essence, everything Priscilla and I had been praying that our Patrick would become.

TURNING THE CORNER

The trials with our Patrick did not end overnight. Priscilla and I withdrew him from the rehab center so we could work with him at home. It was a gutsy step, but it proved to be the correct one.

I took Patrick to San Salvador for a few days to meet Patrick Q. They hit it off and quickly became good friends. Patrick Q. later moved to Dallas, and, as I said we would, we helped him through Bible college. And, as Patrick Q. had promised, he took the time to minister to our son and became instrumental in helping him turn his life in the right direction.

Finally, the blessing had come. After several years of

persevering through this trial, we saw our son released from the bondage of drugs and set on a new path.

To this day, I believe with all my heart that these blessings—for me, my wife, my son, and Patrick Q.—happened because I chose to persevere through the many trials in my life and obey God in doing the things He called me to do as a man of God, businessman, husband, and father. I saw an up-close example of how persevering through even the worst trials this world can throw our way brings blessings in the end.

Trials of all kinds are a fact of life here on earth. But if we persevere through them and continue doing what God has called us to do, then we will receive manifold blessings. What's more, we'll also be changed for the better. That's because God will use our trials to mold us, shape us, and chip away the rough spots. When that happens, we'll be ready to be used for His kingdom's sake.

> Perhaps you can offer someone going through a trial some helpful counsel, but maybe all you can offer is a hearing ear and some time to pray with that person.

SOME PRACTICAL HELP IN PERSEVERING

In a sense, this entire book is about persevering through trials in the business world. I have already given practical helps that I believe can transform your leadership style and even your business itself. Now I want to close this chapter with some practical pointers for the business leader who wants to learn how to persevere in even the toughest of situations.

1. *Seek counsel and support from those who have persevered through trials.* Don't be "macho" and try to fight your way through your struggle on your own. Instead, find godly friends, business associates, pastors, family members—anyone with some spiritual depth and maturity—to give you counsel and support.

2. *Don't wallow in your misery.* One of the great scriptural principles is that when you are seeking the solution to some problem, go out and bless someone with a similar need. Perhaps you can offer someone going through a trial some helpful counsel, but maybe all you can offer is a hearing ear and some time to pray with that person. Either way, you are sure to be a blessing to someone. In doing that, you bless yourself!

3. *If your trial is financial, increase your giving to God.* At points when Priscilla and I faced financial trouble, we increased our giving to the church or ministries we wanted to bless. We did so even when it made better sense, humanly speaking, to use the money for our personal needs. In every instance, God honored our generosity by meeting our needs. I believe that is because we followed a basic principle outlined in scripture: "If you give, you will receive. Your gift will return to you in

full measure, pressed down, shaken together to make room for more" (Luke 6:38 NLT).

Indeed, if you are generous with God, He will be generous with you. This principle works in business, too. If you are the owner of a private enterprise, you have more freedom to give out of your corporate assets. By all means, exercise this privilege and share what you have with God, *especially in tough times*. On the other hand, if you are the leader of a large publicly or privately held firm, there will be corporate and legal restrictions on what you can give. If the company is open to sharing its resources with God, then pursue that avenue with the powers that be. But if you cannot do that, then personally increase your giving to God on behalf of your company. God will honor this approach and bless your generosity—for you *and* for your company.

If you want help in persevering through your trials—even failures—as a business leader, then seek godly counsel, reach out to others, and give. Also, do not live in fear and do not run from the trials. They may not be enjoyable, but if you choose to endure them, then you will emerge with the blessings God has reserved especially for those who persevere.

PRINCIPLE 7:

FOCUS ON THE "BIGGER PICTURE"

He said to them, "Go into all the world and preach the good news to all creation."

MARK 16:15

ONE OF THE THEMES OF THIS
book has been getting God's perspective on any situation, no matter how easy or difficult it may be. That means finding a way to be of the same mind as the Father when it comes to the issues and challenges we face. It means knowing that everything we go through, good or bad, is part of God's plan. It means recognizing that God has an important role for each of us to play in the greatest of *all* plans: redeeming human-kind. And it means being willing to go *where* He wants us to go *when* He wants us to go there.

In short, it means keeping our eyes on God's "bigger picture."

If you can adopt this perspective in life, you will free yourself to enjoy the very best He has for you, even as you are going through difficult times.

FOLLOWING GOD ANYWHERE: A BIBLICAL PRINCIPLE

The Bible contains many examples of people who received God's best simply because they obeyed Him and went where He called them to go when He called them.

Let's take a look at some examples of men of God who focused on the bigger picture.

> Moving business and family hundreds of miles at that time required a staggering leap of faith.

ABRAHAM, THE FATHER OF GOD'S PEOPLE

Abraham, the one God called to be the father of the nation of Israel, was a successful entrepreneur in the agribusiness arena when God called him to move from Ur, in what is now Iraq, to the region of modern-day Israel. This was no easy journey. Moving business and family hundreds of miles at that time, when an area more than a few miles from your home was virtually unknown, required a staggering leap of faith. Abraham had just that kind of faith.

Abraham's obedience meant enduring hardship. When he divided the new land among his family, his nephew Lot chose what appeared to be the best property, leaving Abraham with the leftovers. Not a good start for an agribusinessman! All this time, Abraham and his wife faced struggles on the home front: They wanted children but seemingly could have none.

Despite this adversity, Abraham remained faithful to God and went where He directed when He directed. In the end, Abraham received immense blessings. His business prospered, and his offspring became as numerous as the grains of sand on the beach (see Genesis 22:17).

God had indeed fulfilled His promises to Abraham.

PAUL THE APOSTLE

The New Testament also testifies to the blessings of following God when and where He calls. The book of Acts, for example, is all about going, doing, and sharing the Best News ever. In this book, we read about the apostle Paul, one of the most intrepid travelers who ever lived. After his conversion, Paul followed God's directions and took three major missionary journeys throughout the known world.

In the midst of his journeys, Paul continued to listen to and obey God's direction and "redirection." Acts 16 tells us that he saw a vision in the night to go to Macedonia, part of modern-day Greece, instead of remaining in what we now know as Turkey. Paul obeyed, and because he did, the gospel message reached the first of the Europeans.

> What is the bigger picture for us?

The road was not easy for Paul. He endured some incredible trials, including physical and verbal abuse, imprisonment, poverty, and brutal weather—you name it, and Paul lived it. But he was able to press on for one reason: He knew he was where God wanted him to be.

Abraham and Paul are just a few examples of what godly leaders need to understand: If we are where God wants us to be when He wants us to be there, when we remain focused on His bigger picture, we can lead others through even the most intense challenges and adversities.

What is that bigger picture for us? It is this: Christ will one day return to redeem the earth, but until that happens, we as godly leaders are called to help fulfill the Great Commission of making disciples for Him.

MY OWN BIGGER-PICTURE CALLING

Jesus' call to make disciples has always excited me. Even when I was a boy, I loved hearing from missionaries and dreamed about traveling to many parts of the world so I could tell others about Christ. I believe this is largely because my father and mother pastored a church with a great missions program. Over the years, a steady stream of men and women who worked in every corner of the world—Africa, Asia, Europe, Latin America, as well as North America—passed through our church. Listening to these people's stories fueled my appetite to have a part in fulfilling the Great Commission.

Priscilla also has a strong sense of ministry. She worked for Young Life, the great Christian youth organization, for many years, both as a volunteer and paid staff member. During that time, she developed her own passion for making disciples for Christ.

In a sense, Young Life brought Priscilla into my life. She had moved from her home in the San Francisco Bay area to St. Paul to work full-time for Young Life. After her move, she began attending my family's church and was a regular at the young adult group. We met at one of the group's meetings and were married soon thereafter.

A DESIRE TO TRAVEL

After we were married, Priscilla and I kept our desire to travel and reach others for Christ, despite the fact that in time we became quite busy making a living and raising three sons.

During the early portion of my career—when I was working in public transportation in my hometown of Minneapolis–St. Paul—I longed to travel more, but my job was focused in one place. My interest in global missions remained strong, though, largely because I served on our church's missions committee.

In the early 1980s, my desire to work abroad and in the airline industry grew, and I felt frustrated because nothing in my work life seemed to be moving me in that direction. That all changed when I attended a program called "Cursillo," which the local Lutheran church sponsored in our city. Cursillo is a Christ-centered program that involves, among other things, tangible demonstrations of grace and

> Little did I realize how seriously God would take my words.

love. The name comes from a Spanish word that means "a short course"; in this case, a short course in the deep love of God for each of us.

At the end of the Cursillo program, all the participants were to share with one another what God had said to them or taught them during their time in the program. When it was my time to speak, I stood before the other participants and guests and shared these words of the Old Testament prophet Isaiah: "Then I heard the voice of the Lord saying, 'Whom shall I send? And who will go for us?' And I said, 'Here am I. Send me!' " (Isaiah 6:8). In quoting the prophet, I was not speaking out of frustration over being "stuck" in one place but out of a heartfelt desire to impact the world for God.

> I knew it would be a challenge to land the job, since they typically looked for MBAs from the very best business schools in America.

Little did I realize how seriously God would take my words. Over the course of the next decade and a half, I visited almost every corner of the United States as well as six continents and nearly fifty countries.

THE START OF SOMETHING BIG

Within a few years of my experience with Cursillo, I moved to Dallas with my family, where I took my first job in the private sector. I would be working with a planning and civil engineering consortium on the design and construction of a new urban rail transit system. I was still not in the airline industry, but at least I had taken my first step in a new life in the private sector, where there seemed to be much more career upside.

Eventually, however, our move to Dallas opened for me an unexpected but very welcome door to a career in the airline industry. Through a friend, I secured a contact at American Airlines for a job in its Capacity Planning Group. I knew it would be a challenge to land the job, since they typically looked for MBAs from the very best business schools in America. I didn't have that kind of pedigree, but I moved forward with the application and hiring process anyway.

For what seemed like an eternity, I heard little from American other than the basic requests for a résumé, an application, and references. Finally, one September day, I received a call from a senior human resources person at American, who told me the airline wanted to hire me. There were a few more items to resolve, but I had a solid offer to move into the career I had dreamed about.

MEETING NEW CHALLENGES

The next challenge my "dream career" in the airline industry afforded my family and me was the prospect of a 20 percent salary reduction and a lower-level position than what I held in the consulting firm in which I worked at the time.

As far as American was concerned, it was a "take it or

leave it" offer. My work background did not match American's "profile" for a new hire, but the people at American were intrigued enough with my parallel experience in surface transportation to offer me the position they had. As we thought about the offer, Priscilla and I had to keep reminding ourselves that God was in control of our situation and that somehow He would provide for our family.

I accepted the job and began work in the latter part of 1989. The work was fascinating and in many ways difficult. American was not a friendly place to work. Yes, it was a great laboratory for learning about some of the most advanced techniques in airline profitability analysis, strategic and tactical planning, and flight scheduling. However, I faced life on a smaller salary with the subsequent challenge of supporting my wife and three young sons. I also now had an hour's drive to work versus my previous twenty-minute commute. What's more, less than two years after my arrival at American Airlines, the industry began reeling from the economic downturn in the aftermath of the first Persian Gulf War in 1991. My colleagues and I wondered what was next for us as American went through a couple rounds of layoffs.

> It was on that trip that I faced a very difficult trial, one that would test my resolve in keeping focused on God's bigger picture.

Priscilla and I, my parents, and many dear friends prayed us through these difficult times, and some new friends from church provided some incremental financial assistance, which we needed in order to get by as a family.

I survived the layoffs and began to grasp the new opportunities and projects for me in American Airlines' Capacity Planning Department. I knew that God had me where He wanted me, but I sensed that there was more to come.

PUSHING FORWARD

In 1990, my family and I entered the next major phase on our journey to serving God internationally. As an employee of American Airlines, I was periodically able to use company flight benefits to travel around the country. Our opportunities to travel overseas were limited, but we were able on one occasion to travel to Great Britain to attend the board meeting of a missions organization that ministered in Sri Lanka. It was on that trip that I faced a very difficult trial, one that would test my resolve in keeping focused on God's bigger picture.

Priscilla and I left the children with my parents and headed to the airport, where we waited to see if we, as nonrevenue standby passengers, would get seats on the flight to London. As we waited, I became violently ill. I was feverish, badly chilled, and aching from head to toe. It felt to me like the worst case of flu in human history.

We immediately called some friends and asked them to pray for me. As our friends interceded, I felt as though a force was literally running the length of my body. I felt somewhat better, but the symptoms remained. Not wanting to succumb to this physical attack, Priscilla and I decided to press on.

We got the last two seats on the flight, but to this day I don't remember the eight-and-a-half-hour flight. I was so drained that I slept for the entire trip. Upon reaching London, we met our friends, who drove us ninety minutes north to their home. We stayed at the home of a physician by the name of Julian Pedley. The conference was held in the home of Dr. Sam Muthuveloe. Both men had backgrounds in tropical medicine. Their knowledge and skills proved to be vital.

> I was horrified to discover that 50 percent of my left leg had turned purple and that a darker purple streak seemed to be moving up my femoral artery.

I was exhausted and aching badly, so the Pedleys sent us to a spare bedroom to get some sleep. As I undressed to put on my pajamas, I was horrified to discover that 50 percent of my left leg had turned purple and that a darker purple streak seemed to be moving up my femoral artery. On my left shin was a wound that looked to Priscilla and me like a spider bite.

We surmised that I had been bitten before we left for the airport in Dallas. We had taken a swim in our backyard pool before leaving for the long flight. I had noticed some nasty-looking spiders by the pool on occasion, and, evidently, my leg brushed too close to one that day and it bit me.

The two doctors examined my leg and immediately put me on medications to contain the toxin. I was in much better shape in a few days, but as a result of the bite, I lost the feeling in my left calf and in several toes on my left foot—problems that remain with me to this day.

The episode was an example to Priscilla and me of the importance of persevering in our desire to serve the Lord whenever and wherever He calls us. We could have canceled the trip when I became ill, but we pressed on, believing God was leading us. And because we were obedient—despite what could have been a very real obstacle—God saw us through my illness and moved us along to a new set of opportunities and challenges.

But that wouldn't be the last time I saw the importance of remaining focused on God's bigger picture.

> American gave me a trial assignment: figuring out how to allocate passenger flights between the three airports in Berlin.

THE JOB OF MY DREAMS

In 1993, I had an opportunity to take a position with American Airlines that would fulfill two of my nearly lifelong desires—using my skills in airline planning to work overseas and using my work as the vehicle for ministry. That opportunity came when American started an international consulting group.

American's chairman, Bob Crandall, wanted to give the airline new opportunities to generate revenue from sources other than direct flight operations. Many airlines were still recovering from the economic problems of the post–Gulf War environment, and Mr. Crandall reasoned that since *someone* would help other airlines worldwide as they sought to recover, we should be the ones to provide the help and earn the company incremental income.

When I learned about the new consulting group, I bid for one of the positions and got it. My expertise in capacity planning coupled with my previous consulting experience were just what the group needed. American gave me a trial assignment: figuring out how to allocate passenger flights between the three airports in Berlin. I spoke some German, which proved very useful in reviewing and evaluating the data. I soon became a permanent part of the consulting team.

The following three years turned out to be some of the busiest and most exciting of my work life. The work assignments took me to dozens of countries on six continents. I worked with about twenty-five different airlines and a dozen or so airport authorities. We overhauled airlines, planned new strategic directions for them, set up new route networks, consulted on training of all types, and helped in the design of several airport facilities around the world.

It was interesting work, and it gave me a chance to do what I'd wanted to do all along: travel to other nations, taking the love of God with me.

MORE GOD-ORDAINED CAREER MOVES

Eventually, I had the opportunity to live and work in El

Salvador. Priscilla and I both believed that God had orchestrated this chain of events, for I would not have gotten the job in El Salvador if it had not been for my work experience at American Airlines.

It wasn't three minutes into that conversation that Rabbi Goldstein said something that permanently changed my focus.

There was another part of my personal big picture awaiting me in El Salvador, too, as God planted within me a desire that would later prove to be pivotal in my own work and ministry. This happened on January 2, 2000, when I was invited to have breakfast with a friend and a man I didn't know. Our friend, Mercedes Dalton, had a ministry to Jewish people around the world. She was a native Salvadoran and a dear friend in the Lord. The stranger—at least until that morning—was an Orthodox Jewish rabbi by the name of Yisrael Goldstein.

I had never met an Orthodox Jewish rabbi before, so I thought it would be interesting to have breakfast with him. As it turned out, he was a very likable man, and we hit it off immediately. We struck up a very free and enjoyable conversation, and it wasn't three minutes into that conversation that Rabbi Goldstein said something that permanently changed my focus when it came to work and ministry.

Rabbi Goldstein, who was dressed and groomed completely in the part of an Orthodox Jewish rabbi, looked at me and pointed his finger at me as only a rabbi can and said, "You know, it is the responsibility of you Christians to help bring us Jews back to God!"

Rabbi Goldstein's words shook me up, and they sparked what until then had been a casual interest in the people of Israel. I felt his words were God's way of saying to me, "Whatever you do in the future needs to point to Israel."

Rabbi Goldstein's words—and the thoughts that followed—stayed with me, even as I realized it was time for me to leave El Salvador and seek employment with a U.S.-based airline. As I prayed about finding a new position, God impressed upon me the need to be in a place where I could be a blessing to the people in Israel and where I could learn to better understand the Jewish roots of my faith.

SEEKING AND FINDING AN "ISRAEL CONNECTION"

One day during my job search, I contacted a young man who had worked for me in El Salvador but who had left to work for a major aircraft leasing company. At my request, he agreed to pass my résumé to his boss, the owner of the company. Within a matter of hours, I received a return call at my office in San Salvador asking me to meet the owner at a hotel in Miami to discuss a job as CEO of Vanguard Airlines, in which he had a significant stake.

I was definitely interested in meeting him, but I had some conditions for employment, namely, the "Israel connection" I believed God had put on my and Priscilla's hearts. So as I prayed about the upcoming interview, I asked God to confirm His word to me and show me a linkage between this possible job as an airline CEO and His desire for us to be involved with Israel.

The meeting in Miami went very well, and a few days later I found myself in Kansas City at Vanguard's headquarters, where I met with the staff with whom I would be working. I talked first with the vice president of maintenance and engineering. I knew that small airlines like Vanguard contracted with third parties for heavy maintenance because it was not cost effective to do it internally.

> At that moment, I was convinced that this was the Israel connection I had sought.

"Where does Vanguard do its heavy maintenance?" I asked him.

"Well," he replied, "we send our engines and avionics to Israel for overhaul."

Those words brought tears to my eyes. At that moment, I was convinced that this was the Israel connection I had sought. To me, it represented the confirmation I needed before taking the job with Vanguard. With this confirmation under our belts, I settled into Kansas City in May 2001.

This episode in our lives demonstrated to us that if we take time to seek God for direction, He is more than able to speak to us and give us confirmation. It also was a demonstration of the blessings we receive when we seek, listen, and obey Him and His will for us when it comes to His bigger-picture program.

My experiences have brought me to the point where I can say with certainty that godly leaders need to have a bigger-picture focus if they want to lead in a way that pleases God.

Next, I want to cover some key points for doing just that.

Some Pointers on Having a Big-Picture Focus

Becoming a part of God's big picture is the most important thing you can do as a leader. But it might surprise you to know that it's a lot simpler than many would think. It's just a matter of following some simple steps:

1. *Be willing to go where God leads you and do what He wants you to do.* One thing I have observed, both in my life as a leader and in the lives of others, is that the first step in leading with a big-picture focus is having a willingness to obey God and His leading.

> One of the keys to adopting a heart of obedience is getting through our heads that God wants more than anything to bless us.

We need to have an attitude that says, "God, wherever You want me to go and whatever You want me to do, I'll do it, because I know You want to bless me and those around me." Sadly, many leaders have that all backwards, taking instead an attitude that says, "God, You tell me what You want me to do, and if I think it works for me, then I'll do it."

One of the keys to adopting a heart of obedience is getting through our heads that God wants more than anything to bless us. God says this very plainly: "Oh, that their hearts would be inclined to fear me and keep all my commands always, so that it might go well with them and their children forever!" (Deuteronomy 5:29).

So before you start seeking what God has for you, make sure you are willing to hear Him and obey!

2. *Ask God where He wants you to go, when He wants you to go there, and what He wants you to do once you get there.* Sadly, many people who desire more than anything to follow God's leading are frozen in place because they don't know where He wants them to go or what He wants them to do. But finding out what He wants from us isn't as complicated as many of us try to make it. In fact, most of the time it's just a matter of asking.

The apostle James gives us some good pointers for asking for direction:

> *If any of you lacks wisdom, he should ask God, who gives generously to all without finding fault, and it will be given to him. But when he asks, he must believe and not doubt, because he who doubts is like a wave of the sea, blown and tossed by the wind. That man should not think he will receive anything from the Lord.*
>
> JAMES 1:5–7

In short, ask God in faith for direction, and He'll give it to you!

But how does He give it? I have learned that God lets us know where He wants us to be and when in any number of ways —through prayer alone with Him or with others we trust, through His written Word, and through godly counsel. I believe He'll use the way He knows works best for each of us as individuals.

3. *Find out your heart's desires.* A lot of godly leaders have a hard time buying into this, but it's true: Oftentimes, we can find God's will for us by simply examining our hearts and finding out what He's put in there for us.

Ask God what He wants from you—the wheres, whens, and whats alike.

That's not as fleshly or "me-focused" as it might sound at first. You see, when we submit ourselves to God and make ourselves available to be a part of His bigger-picture plans, we are then ready to receive His direction and leading. When that happens, His desires become our desires. Then obedience becomes a matter of doing the things for His kingdom that are important to us.

This is partly what the psalmist meant when he wrote, "Delight yourself in the LORD, and he will give you the desires of your heart" (Psalm 37:4).

So when you ask God what He wants from you—the

wheres, whens, and whats alike—ask Him to make those very things more important to you than anything else.

4. *Seek confirmation.* Once you've decided to follow God's leading and have gotten what you believe is His plan for you, then take this step: Get some confirmation. For some people, getting confirmation like this might sound a little too "charismatic." But seeking confirmation is a scriptural principle that all believers should follow. In fact, it's a principle that has taken on its own name: "putting out a fleece."

The principle of "putting out a fleece" comes from the Old Testament, specifically Judges 6, where we read of God's call to Gideon to lead the people of Israel in battle against a host of enemies. Gideon had an inkling that God wanted him to lead his people in battle, but he wanted some confirmation. So instead of just going out to save Israel, Gideon asked God for a sign: He would lay out a sheep's fleece, and if on the following morning there was dew on the fleece but not on the ground around it, that would confirm God's calling.

That's exactly what happened, too. But Gideon wanted to take this confirmation one more step. He would again lay out the fleece, and if the following morning it was dry while the ground around it was wet with dew, then that would be all the confirmation he needed. Sure enough, the next morning the fleece was bone-dry while the ground around it was soaked with dew.

When you believe that God is leading you in some

particular direction but you want confirmation, ask Him. He won't be offended, and I believe He'll certainly give it to you.

5. *Press forward in accomplishing your part in God's big picture, even when you face obstacles.* We need to understand that being completely committed to living and serving according to God's bigger picture doesn't mean that everything will always go smoothly or easily. As I've pointed out in this book, trials and tests are going to be a part of our lives as godly leaders.

But we can persevere through the difficult time if we simply focus on these bigger-picture principles:

God is bigger than any of our problems.

God is in control, even when life seems out of control.

God has our enemy on a short leash and won't allow him to push us beyond what we're able to bear.

Our trials and tests are a part of His program.

Knowing these things, you can persevere even in the toughest of times. So keep your focus on God and on His bigger picture. Ask Him to show you the specifics of what your involvement in that bigger picture looks like. And above all. . .

Never give up!

AUTHOR BIO

Scott Dickson is a senior airline executive with thirty years of experience who has worked with airlines, airports, and tourism groups on six continents and in fifty countries.

In his current responsibilities as president of Airline Partner Services, Scott and his team provide value-added marketing, charter brokering, and management services to a select group of airlines in the Americas.

Scott has also served as chairman of the board, president, and CEO of Vanguard Airlines. Vanguard Airlines operated a fleet of fifteen aircraft from its hub in Kansas City, with a staff of eleven hundred, providing value-priced service between eighteen major U.S. cities. Prior to joining Vanguard, Scott served as VP of Planning and Revenue Management for the Central American–based airline Grupo TACA. He also held positions with several AMR Corporation units including American Airlines, AMR Consulting, and SABRE Inc.

Scott earned both his Master of Arts and Bachelor of Arts degrees in Urban and Transport Geography from the University of Minnesota. He is a member of the Institute of Transportation Engineers.

Scott and his wife, Priscilla, reside in the Dallas, Texas, area. They have three adult sons, two grandchildren, and an exceedingly spoiled dog. The Dicksons are active in their church and numerous mission outreach endeavors. Scott serves as a board member with the international ministry Global Action. Scott and Priscilla also direct their own mission organization, A.D. Outreach.

ACKNOWLEDGMENTS

The practical helps offered in *Never Give Up* to leaders facing stressful business situations have been developed and honed through shared experiences with colleagues throughout the transportation industry as well as with my family.

As such, I am deeply grateful to dear friends and colleagues at the many airlines where I spent time, particularly American Airlines, Grupo TACA, Vanguard Airlines, and Lloyd Aeréo Boliviano. My all-too-brief twenty months at Vanguard Airlines holds special significance as it brought into focus the essence of this book. I pray that the former Vanguard staff members experience the richest of God's blessings in their new endeavors.

I am equally indebted to the men and women of the old Metropolitan Transit Commission of Minneapolis–St. Paul, now known as the Transit Operating Division of the Metropolitan Council, where I cut my teeth as a manager. It was there, in my first career experience, that I felt encouraged to put into practice a number of the management ideas God taught me.

Many thanks also goes to coauthors Mark Littleton and Tracy Sumner who used their considerable writing talent and organizational skills to bring this book to completion. They also get kudos for putting up with my extensive travels between Texas, Florida, and Bolivia as we sought to meet deadlines.

Indeed, this book was completed while I was in the city of Cochabamba, Bolivia, high up in the Andes Mountains where my colleagues at Lloyd Aeréo Boliviano make their headquarters.

Finally, my family was also instrumental in shaping this book, and my life, by helping me grow in my faith and career. My parents, Bob and Gloria Dickson, and sister, Leslie, during their extensive ministry at Hope Presbyterian Church in Minneapolis, modeled Jesus' love for me at an early age. I also owe a great thanks to them, especially my father, for stimulating my love of aviation as I listened to his stories about serving as a member of a B-29 bomber crew at the end of World War II.

My wife, Priscilla, gets the last word. I have the greatest partner for life. I have learned so much from her about the power of prayer and the power of affirming God's promises, and I have been richly blessed by her insights into the hearts of others. She has been so patient and supportive of my globe-hopping. What a joy to share my life with her, our sons, daughters-in-law, and grandchildren.

Also from Barbour Publishing

Living Life to the Max
by Vernon Armitage and Mark Littleton
Through insightful scriptures, relevant examples, and practical applications, *Living Life to the Max* puts at readers' fingertips God's how-to principles for living the life He created to the fullest.
ISBN 1-59310-066-3
224 pages

Living a Life of Hope
by Nathan Busenitz
Living a Life of Hope helps readers shift their gaze from the "here and now" to the wonders of "forever" for a life of greater purpose, power, and joy.
ISBN 1-58660-983-1
256 pages

Outdoors with God
by Lance Moore
Quiet-time inspiration finds truth in God's Word— and nature.
ISBN 1-58660-919-X
224 pages

Men Are Clams, Women Are Crowbars
by David Clarke, PhD
Dr. David Clarke details the divergent ways men and women approach emotional issues, then offers solutions for couples who want to bridge the gender gap.
ISBN 1-58660-726-X
256 pages